Communication Media Testing

EC-Council | Press

Volume 4 of 5 mapping to

E | CSA™

EC-Council | Certified Security Analyst

Certification

COURSE TECHNOLOGY
CENGAGE Learning™

Australia • Brazil • Japan • Korea • Mexico • Singapore • Spain • United Kingdom • United States

COURSE TECHNOLOGY
CENGAGE Learning™

Communication Media Testing
EC-Council | Press

Course Technology/Cengage Learning Staff:

Vice President, Career and Professional Editorial: Dave Garza

Director of Learning Solutions: Matthew Kane

Executive Editor: Stephen Helba

Managing Editor: Marah Bellegarde

Editorial Assistant: Meghan Orvis

Vice President, Career and Professional Marketing: Jennifer Ann Baker

Marketing Director: Deborah Yarnell

Marketing Manager: Erin Coffin

Marketing Coordinator: Shanna Gibbs

Production Director: Carolyn Miller

Production Manager: Andrew Crouth

Content Project Manager: Brooke Greenhouse

Senior Art Director: Jack Pendleton

EC-Council:

President | EC-Council: Sanjay Bavisi

Sr. Director US | EC-Council: Steven Graham

For product information and technology assistance, contact us at
Cengage Learning Customer & Sales Support, 1-800-354-9706

For permission to use material from this text or product, submit all requests online at **www.cengage.com/permissions**. Further permissions questions can be e-mailed to **permissionrequest@cengage.com**

Library of Congress Control Number: 2010928442

ISBN-13: 978-1-4354-8369-9

ISBN-10: 1-4354-8369-3

Cengage Learning
5 Maxwell Drive
Clifton Park, NY 12065-2919
USA

Cengage Learning is a leading provider of customized learning solutions with office locations around the globe, including Singapore, the United Kingdom, Australia, Mexico, Brazil, and Japan. Locate your local office at: **international.cengage.com/region**

Cengage Learning products are represented in Canada by Nelson Education, Ltd.

For more learning solutions, please visit our corporate website at **www.cengage.com**

NOTICE TO THE READER

Printed in the United States of America
1 2 3 4 5 6 7 13 12 11 10

Brief Table of Contents

Table of Contents

Hacking and electronic crimes sophistication has grown at an exponential rate in recent years. In fact, recent reports have indicated that cyber crime already surpasses the illegal drug trade! Unethical hackers better known as *black hats* are preying on information systems of government, corporate, public, and private networks and are constantly testing the security mechanisms of these organizations to the limit with the sole aim of exploiting it and profiting from the exercise. High profile crimes have proven that the traditional approach to computer security is simply not sufficient, even with the strongest perimeter, properly configured defense mechanisms like firewalls, intrusion detection, and prevention systems, strong end-to-end encryption standards, and anti-virus software. Hackers have proven their dedication and ability to systematically penetrate networks all over the world. In some cases *black hats* may be able to execute attacks so flawlessly that they can compromise a system, steal everything of value, and completely erase their tracks in less than 20 minutes!

The EC-Council Press is dedicated to stopping hackers in their tracks.

About EC-Council

The International Council of Electronic Commerce Consultants, better known as EC-Council was founded in late 2001 to address the need for well-educated and certified information security and e-business practitioners. EC-Council is a global, member-based organization comprised of industry and subject matter experts all working together to set the standards and raise the bar in information security certification and education.

EC-Council first developed the *Certified Ethical Hacker,* C|EH program. The goal of this program is to teach the methodologies, tools, and techniques used by hackers. Leveraging the collective knowledge from hundreds of subject matter experts, the C|EH program has rapidly gained popularity around the globe and is now delivered in over 70 countries by over 450 authorized training centers. Over 60,000 information security practitioners have been trained.

C|EH is the benchmark for many government entities and major corporations around the world. Shortly after C|EH was launched, EC-Council developed the *Certified Security Analyst,* E|CSA. The goal of the E|CSA program is to teach groundbreaking analysis methods that must be applied while conducting advanced penetration testing. E|CSA leads to the *Licensed Penetration Tester,* L|PT status. The *Computer Hacking Forensic Investigator,* C|HFI was formed with the same design methodologies above and has become a global standard in certification for computer forensics. EC-Council through its impervious network of professionals, and huge industry following has developed various other programs in information security and e-business. EC-Council Certifications are viewed as the essential certifications needed where standard configuration and security policy courses fall short. Providing a true, hands-on, tactical approach to security, individuals armed with the knowledge disseminated by EC-Council programs are securing networks around the world and beating the hackers at their own game.

About the EC-Council | Press

The EC-Council | Press was formed in late 2008 as a result of a cutting edge partnership between global information security certification leader, EC-Council and leading global academic publisher, Cengage Learning. This partnership marks a revolution in academic textbooks and courses of study in Information Security, Computer Forensics, Disaster Recovery, and End-User Security. By identifying the essential topics and content of EC-Council professional certification programs, and repurposing this world class content to fit academic programs, the EC-Council | Press was formed. The academic community is now able to incorporate this powerful cutting edge content into new and existing Information Security programs. By closing the gap between academic study and professional certification, students and instructors are able to leverage the power of rigorous academic focus and high demand industry certification. The EC-Council | Press is set to revolutionize global information security programs and ultimately create a new breed of practitioners capable of combating the growing epidemic of cybercrime and the rising threat of cyber-war.

Penetration Testing Series

The EC-Council | Press *Penetration Testing* series, preparing learners for E|CSA/LPT certification, is intended for those studying to become Network Server Administrators, Firewall Administrators, Security Testers, System Administrators and Risk Assessment professionals. This series covers a broad base of topics in advanced penetration testing and security analysis. The content of this program is designed to expose the learner to groundbreaking methodologies in conducting thorough security analysis, as well as advanced penetration testing techniques. Armed with the knowledge from the Penetration Testing series, learners will be able to perform the intensive assessments required to effectively identify and mitigate risks to the security of the organization's infrastructure. The series when used in its entirety helps prepare learners to take and succeed on the E|CSA, Certified Security Analyst certification exam.

Books in Series
- *Penetration Testing: Security Analysis*/1435483669
- *Penetration Testing: Procedures and Methodologies*/1435483677
- *Penetration Testing: Network and Perimeter Testing*/1435483685
- *Penetration Testing: Communication Media Testing*/1435483693
- *Penetration Testing: Network Threat Testing*/1435483707

Communication Media Testing

Communication Media Testing coverage includes penetration testing of wireless networks, VoIPs, VPNs, Bluetooth and handheld devices, telecommunication and broadband communication systems.

Chapter Contents

Chapter 1, *Wireless Network Penetration Testing*, topic coverage includes rogue access points, wireless network traffic, WEP keys, wireless signals, and encrypted packets. Chapter 2, *Advanced Wireless Testing*, discusses NetStumbler, active and passive WLAN detection, and air-crack-ng. Chapter 3, *VoIP Penetration Testing*, explains how test a VoIP system for many known vulnerabilities. Chapter 4, *VPN Penetration Testing*, discusses how to perform tests on both IPSec and SSL VPNs. Chapter 5, *Wardialing*, explains how to perform a wardialing penetration test along with a discussion on the tools used in this type of testing. Chapter 6, *Bluetooth and Handheld Device Penetration Testing*, includes coverage of iPhone and iPod, BlackBerry, PDA's and Bluetooth testing. Chapter 7, *Telecommunication and Broadband Communication Penetration Testing*, includes testing of cable modem networks, DSL networks and satellite broadband service.

Chapter Features

Many features are included in each chapter and all are designed to enhance the learner's learning experience. Features include:

- *Objectives* begin each chapter and focus the learner on the most important concepts in the chapter.

- *Key Terms* are designed to familiarize the learner with terms that will be used within the chapter.

- *Chapter Summary*, at the end of each chapter, serves as a review of the key concepts covered in the chapter.

- *Review Questions* allow the learner to test their comprehension of the chapter content.

- *Hands-On Projects* encourage the learner to apply the knowledge they have gained after finishing the chapter. Chapters covering the Licensed Penetration Testing (LPT) materials do not have Hands-On Projects. The LPT content does not lend itself to these types of activities. Files for the *Hands-On Projects* can be found on the Student Resource Center. Note: you will need your access code provided in your book to enter the site. Visit *www.cengage.com/community/eccouncil* for a link to the Student Resource Center.

Student Resource Center

The Student Resource Center contains all the files you need to complete the Hands-On Projects found at the end of the chapters. Chapters covering the Licensed Penetration Testing (LPT) materials do not have Hands-On Projects. The LPT content does not lend itself to these types of activities. Access the Student Resource Center with the access code provided in your book. Instructions for logging onto the Student Resource Site are included with the access code. Visit *www.cengage.com/community/eccouncil* for a link to the Student Resource Center.

Additional Instructor Resources

Free to all instructors who adopt the *Communication Media Testing* book for their courses is a complete package of instructor resources. These resources are available from the Course Technology web site, *www.cengage.com/coursetechnology*, by going to the product page for this book in the online catalog, click on the Companion Site on the Faculty side; click on any of the Instructor Resources in the left navigation and login to access the files. Once you accept the license agreement, the selected files will be displayed.

Resources include:

- *Instructor Manual*: This manual includes course objectives and additional information to help your instruction.

- *ExamView Testbank*: This Windows-based testing software helps instructors design and administer tests and pre-tests. In addition to generating tests that can be printed and administered, this full-featured program has an online testing component that allows students to take tests at the computer and have their exams automatically graded.

- *PowerPoint Presentations*: This book comes with a set of Microsoft PowerPoint slides for each chapter. These slides are meant to be used as a teaching aid for classroom presentations, to be made available to students for chapter review, or to be printed for classroom distribution. Instructors are also at liberty to add their own slides.

- *Labs*: Additional Hands-on Activities to provide additional practice for your students.

- *Assessment Activities*: Additional assessment opportunities including discussion questions, writing assignments, internet research activities, and homework assignments along with a final cumulative project.

- *Final Exam*: Provides a comprehensive assessment of *Communication Media Testing* content.

Cengage Learning Information Security Community Site

This site was created for learners and instructors to find out about the latest in information security news and technology.
Visit *community.cengage.com/infosec* to:

- Learn what's new in information security through live news feeds, videos and podcasts.

- Connect with your peers and security experts through blogs and forums.

- Browse our online catalog.

How to Become E|CSA Certified

EC-Council Certified Security Analyst (E|CSA) complements the Certified Ethical Hacker (C|EH) certification by exploring the analytical phase of ethical hacking. While C|EH exposes the learner to hacking tools and technologies, E|CSA takes it a step further by exploring how to analyze the outcome from these tools and technologies.

E|CSA is a relevant milestone towards achieving EC-Council's Licensed Penetration Tester (LPT), which also ingrains the learner in the business aspect of penetration testing. The LPT standardizes the knowledge base for penetration testing professionals by incorporating the best practices followed by experienced experts in the field.

The LPT designation is achieved via an application/approval process. LPT is obtained by holding both the CEH and ECSA, then completing the application process for LPT found here at *http://www.eccouncil.org/lpt.htm*.

ElCSA Certification exams are available through Authorized Prometric Testing Centers. To finalize your certification after your training, you must:

1. Apply for and Purchase an exam voucher from the EC-Council Community Site at Cengage: *www.cengage.com/community/eccouncil*.

2. Once you have your Exam Voucher, visit *www.prometric.com* and schedule your exam.

3. Take and pass the ElCSA certification examination with a score of 70% or better.

About Our Other EC-Council | Press Products

Ethical Hacking and Countermeasures Series

The EC-Council | Press *Ethical Hacking and Countermeasures* series is intended for those studying to become security officers, auditors, security professionals, site administrators, and anyone who is concerned about or responsible for the integrity of the network infrastructure. The series includes a broad base of topics in offensive network security, ethical hacking, as well as network defense and countermeasures. The content of this series is designed to immerse the learner into an interactive environment where they will be shown how to scan, test, hack and secure information systems. A wide variety of tools, viruses, and malware is presented in these books, providing a complete understanding of the tactics and tools used by hackers. By gaining a thorough understanding of how hackers operate, ethical hackers are able to set up strong countermeasures and defensive systems to protect their organization's critical infrastructure and information. The series when used in its entirety helps prepare readers to take and succeed on the ClEH certification exam from EC-Council.

Books in Series
- *Ethical Hacking and Countermeasures: Attack Phases*/143548360X
- *Ethical Hacking and Countermeasures: Threats and Defense Mechanisms*/1435483618
- *Ethical Hacking and Countermeasures: Web Applications and Data Servers*/1435483626
- *Ethical Hacking and Countermeasures: Linux, Macintosh and Mobile Systems*/1435483642
- *Ethical Hacking and Countermeasures: Secure Network Infrastructures*/1435483650

Computer Forensics Series

The EC-Council | Press *Computer Forensics* series, preparing learners for ClHFI certification, is intended for those studying to become police investigators and other law enforcement personnel, defense and military personnel, e-business security professionals, systems administrators, legal professionals, banking, insurance and other professionals, government agencies, and IT managers. The content of this program is designed to expose the learner to the process of detecting attacks and collecting evidence in a forensically sound manner with the intent to report crime and prevent future attacks. Advanced techniques in computer investigation and analysis with interest in generating potential legal evidence are included. In full, this series prepares the learner to identify evidence in computer related crime and abuse cases as well as track the intrusive hacker's path through client system.

Books in Series
- *Computer Forensics: Investigation Procedures and Response*/1435483499
- *Computer Forensics: Investigating Hard Disks, File and Operating Systems*/1435483502
- *Computer Forensics: Investigating Data and Image Files*/1435483510
- *Computer Forensics: Investigating Network Intrusions and Cybercrime*/1435483529
- *Computer Forensics: Investigating Wireless Networks and Devices*/1435483537

Network Defense Series

The EC-Council | Press *Network Defense* series, preparing learners for ElNSA certification, is intended for those studying to become system administrators, network administrators and anyone who is interested in network security technologies. This series is designed to educate learners, from a vendor neutral standpoint, how to defend the networks they manage. This series covers the fundamental skills in evaluating internal and external threats to network security, design, and how to enforce network level security policies, and ultimately protect an organization's information. Covering a broad range of topics from secure network fundamentals, protocols & analysis, standards and policy, hardening infrastructure, to configuring IPS, IDS and firewalls, bastion host and honeypots, among many other topics, learners completing this series will have a full understanding of defensive measures taken to secure their organizations information. The series when used in its entirety helps prepare readers to take and succeed on the E|NSA, Network Security Administrator certification exam from EC-Council.

Books in Series
- *Network Defense: Fundamentals and Protocols*/1435483553
- *Network Defense: Security Policy and Threats*/1435483561
- *Network Defense: Perimeter Defense Mechanisms*/143548357X
- *Network Defense: Securing and Troubleshooting Network Operating Systems*/1435483588
- *Network Defense: Security and Vulnerability Assessment*/1435483596

Cyber Safety/1435483715

Cyber Safety is designed for anyone who is interested in learning computer networking and security basics. This product provides information cyber crime; security procedures; how to recognize security threats and attacks, incident response, and how to secure internet access. This book gives individuals the basic security literacy skills to begin high-end IT programs. The book also prepares readers to take and succeed on the Security|5 certification exam from EC-Council.

Wireless Safety/1435483766

Wireless Safety introduces the learner to the basics of wireless technologies and its practical adaptation. *Wireless|5* is tailored to cater to any individual's desire to learn more about wireless technology. It requires no pre-requisite knowledge and aims to educate the learner in simple applications of these technologies. Topics include wireless signal propagation, IEEE and ETSI Wireless Standards, WLANs and Operation, Wireless Protocols and Communication Languages, Wireless Devices, and Wireless Security Network The book also prepares readers to take and succeed on the Wireless|5 certification exam from EC-Council.

Network Safety/1435483774

Network Safety provides the basic core knowledge on how infrastructure enables a working environment. Intended for those in an office environment and for the home user who wants to optimize resource utilization, share infrastructure and make the best of technology and the convenience it offers. Topics include foundations of networks, networking components, wireless networks, basic hardware components, the networking environment and connectivity as well as troubleshooting. The book also prepares readers to take and succeed on the Network|5 certification exam from EC-Council.

Disaster Recovery Series

The *Disaster Recovery Series* is designed to fortify virtualization technology knowledge of system administrators, systems engineers, enterprise system architects, and any IT professional who is concerned about the integrity of the their network infrastructure. Virtualization technology gives the advantage of additional flexibility as well as cost savings while deploying a disaster recovery solution. The series when used in its entirety helps prepare readers to take and succeed on the E|CDR and E|CVT, Disaster Recovery and Virtualization Technology certification exam from EC-Council. The EC-Council Certified Disaster Recovery and Virtualization Technology professional will have a better understanding of how to setup Disaster Recovery Plans using traditional and virtual technologies to ensure business continuity in the event of a disaster.

Books in Series
- *Disaster Recovery*/1435488709
- *Virtualization Security*/1435488695

Acknowledgements

Michael H. Goldner is the Chair of the School of Information Technology for ITT Technical Institute in Norfolk Virginia, and also teaches bachelor level courses in computer network and information security systems. Michael has served on and chaired ITT Educational Services Inc. National Curriculum Committee on Information Security. He received his Juris Doctorate from Stetson University College of Law, his undergraduate degree from Miami University and has been working over fifteen years in the area of Information Technology. He is an active member of the American Bar Association, and has served on that organization's Cyber Law committee. He is a member of IEEE, ACM and ISSA, and is the holder of a number of industrially recognized certifications including, CISSP, CEH, CHFI, CEI, MCT, MCSE/Security, Security+, Network+ and A+. Michael recently completed the design and creation of a computer forensic program for ITT Technical Institute, and has worked closely with both EC-Council and Delmar/Cengage Learning in the creation of this EC-Council Press series.

## Chapter 1

Wireless Network Penetration Testing

Objectives

After completing this chapter, you should be able to:

- Discover rogue access points
- Sniff wireless network traffic
- Crack WEP keys
- Jam wireless signals
- Attempt a man-in-the-middle attack
- Generate large amounts of network
- Inject encrypted packets

Key Terms

Jammer   device used to block wireless network communication within a specific area

MAC flooding   a computer network enumeration and footprinting technique (attack) that involves the spoofing of a network interface's unique MAC address

Man-in-the middle (MITM) attack   an attack in which the attacker intercepts packets, reads or alters them, and then sends them on to their proper destination

Media access control (MAC) address   a unique address that is specific to a system

Rogue access points   WAPs that are unauthorized by the network administrator

Sniffer   a network protocol analyzer that identifies the type of protocol utilized, the IP, the server name, and the host associated with a packet

Wireless access point (WAP)   a device used to access a wireless network

Introduction to Wireless Network Penetration Testing

Wireless networks are often overlooked when considering a security policy. However, wireless networks are becoming more and more common as companies and organizations use them to enhance workplace productivity. These networks, if hacked, can be used to obtain personal financial information from intercepted e-mails. They can also be used to find information that will aid an attack on the larger network. This chapter teaches you how to perform wireless network penetration testing.

Security Policy Assessment

After initially setting up a wireless network, the organization should develop and assess a security policy. After this is done, the network should be tested. The following steps should be taken to perform a wireless assessment:

- Establish a security baseline for all equipment.
- Create a network diagram and list of all equipment.
- Check each piece of equipment for compliance with the baseline.
- Gather specific firmware versions for each piece of equipment.
- Determine if security problems exist in any of the firmware versions currently deployed.
- Check for any unnecessary services on the equipment.
- Discover any unauthorized access points.
- Determine the maximum distance that wireless traffic can be received from each access point.
- Verify that unencrypted traffic is not traversing the wireless network.
- Verify that weak forms of WEP are not in use.
- Document deficiencies and begin to plan corrections.

Wireless Monitoring

Wireless monitoring is a passive approach to testing wireless networks that allows an administrator to determine if a network has any obvious security flaws. A wireless monitoring tool, such as WirelessMon (Figure 1-1), allows the administrator to perform the following tasks:

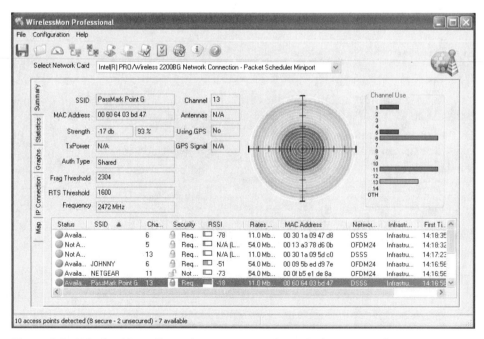

Figure 1-1   WirelessMon allows the user to monitor wireless networks.

- Examine the condition of the wireless adapter.
- Collect information about neighborhood wireless access points in real time.
- Collect information about hot spots in real time.
- Verify wireless network configuration.
- Test all the wireless network devices and hardware.
- Test the local access points' security settings.

Wireless Penetration Testing Steps

- *Step 1*: Discover rogue access points.
- *Step 2*: Sniff the traffic between the AP and linked devices.
- *Step 3*: Verify encryption.
- *Step 4*: Crack static WEP keys.
- *Step 5*: Brute-force keys using Aircrack.
- *Step 6*: Spoof a MAC address.
- *Step 7*: Jam the signal.
- *Step 8*: Sniff the wireless traffic.
- *Step 9*: Attempt a man-in-the-middle attack.
- *Step 10*: Attempt rapid traffic generation.
- *Step 11*: Try to inject an encrypted packet.
- *Step 12*: Attempt single-packet decryption.
- *Step 13*: Document everything.

Step 1: Discover Rogue Access Points

Wireless access points (WAPs) are devices used to access a wireless network. *Rogue access points* are those WAPs that are unauthorized by the network administrator. Rogue access point detection consists of two steps: detecting WAPs and checking them to see if they are rogue access points. The following can be used to detect WAPs:

- *Scanners*: Testers can use a radio frequency (RF) scanning tool, such as PowerScan RF, to identify any wireless device operating in the network area. An RF scanning tool uses sensors to detect wireless devices. The drawback of this kind of tool is that the sensors have a limited range. If the rogue access point is outside of the coverage area, then it will not be detected.
- *Software*: Programs such as AirSnort and NetStumbler can be used to detect all WAPs within the network range.

Once a WAP is detected, the next step is to identify whether or not it is a rogue access point. One way to do this is to use a preconfigured authorized list of WAPs. Any newly detected WAP that falls outside the authorized list would be tagged as a rogue. Lists can be developed in the following ways:

- *Authorized MAC*: Administrators can import ACL settings into the WiFi Manager tool or type in the MAC address of authorized access points on the network. This enables the rogue detection tool to alert WLAN administrators whenever a WAP with an unauthorized MAC is detected.
- *Authorized SSID*: Enterprises would, in most cases, standardize the authorized SSIDs that need to be used. These SSIDs can be fed to a rogue detection tool so that it alerts WLAN administrators whenever a WAP with an unauthorized SSID is detected.
- *Authorized vendor*: Many enterprises standardize their WLAN gear and prefer to add devices only from those vendors as they grow. This enables a rogue detection tool to alert WLAN administrators whenever a WAP from a vendor other than the standard one is detected.

- *Authorized radio media type*: Enterprises sometimes standardize on 802.11a, b, g, or bg WAPs. This enables a rogue detection tool to alert WLAN administrators whenever a WAP with a different radio media type is detected.
- *Authorized channel*: Sometimes, enterprises may want their WAPs to operate on select channels. This enables the rogue detection tool to alert WLAN administrators whenever a WAP operating on a different channel is detected.

Step 2: Sniff the Traffic Between the AP and Linked Devices

Testers can use the BackTrack tool to determine which devices are linked with the wireless access point and to capture information within range. They can also use the Airodump tool to get the MAC address of the WAP, as shown in Figure 1-2.

Step 3: Verify Encryption

In a wireless network, encryption may change depending on the type of connection. There are four major types of encryption that should be checked during a penetration test:

1. Wired Equivalent Privacy (WEP)
2. Wi-Fi Protected Access (WPA)
3. Wi-Fi Protected Access 2 (WPA2)
4. Extensible Authentication Protocol (EAP)

The first step, however, is to check for traffic that is not encrypted. Checking for unencrypted traffic can be done with AiroPeek, as shown in Figure 1-3.

Step 4: Crack Static WEP Keys

WEP is a component of the IEEE 802.11 WLAN standards. Its primary purpose is to provide for confidentiality of data on wireless networks at a level equivalent to that of wired LANs. 802.11 WEP encrypts data only between 802.11 stations. WEP uses shared secret keys of 40 or 104 bits to encrypt and decrypt data.

WEP keys can be cracked using AirSnort, as shown in Figure 1-4. AirSnort is a wireless LAN (WLAN) tool that recovers encryption keys on 802.11b WEP networks. AirSnort operates by passively monitoring transmissions and computing the encryption key when enough packets have been gathered. AirSnort runs on Windows or Linux, and requires that the wireless network interface card (NIC) is capable of RF monitor mode

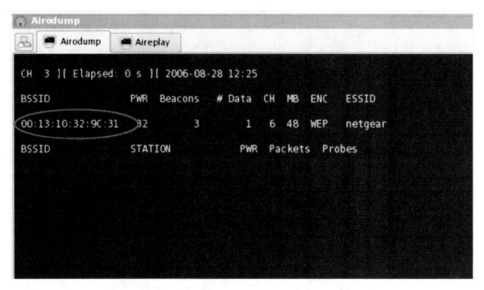

Figure 1-2   Airodump can provide the MAC address of a wireless access point.

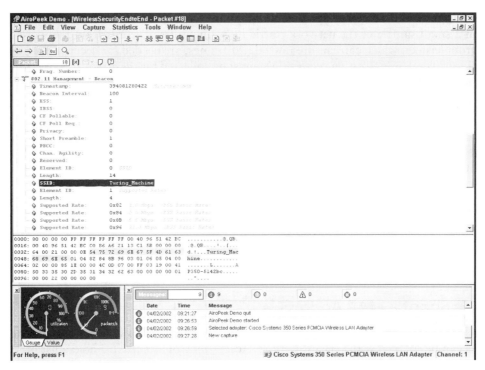

Figure 1-3   AiroPeek allows the user to check for unencrypted traffic.

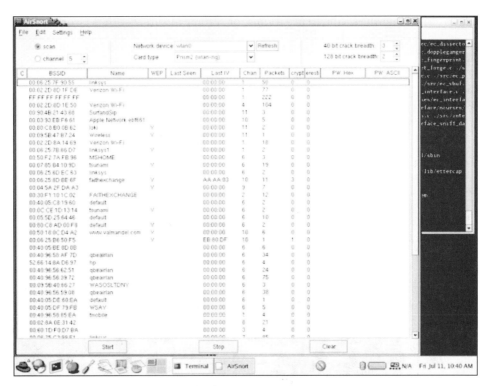

Figure 1-4   WEP keys can be cracked using AirSnort.

and that it passes monitor mode packets up via the PF_PACKET interface. AirSnort performs a dictionary attack on a small sample of the network traffic by trying a list of words from the word list. Packet dumps like those from Kismet, which can capture raw 802.11 frames, are needed for decryption. Between 1,200 and 4,000 packets with weak initialization vectors (IVs) must be collected for the attack to work. Out of 16 million possible IVs, approximately 9,000 of them are weak.

Step 5: Brute-Force Keys Using Aircrack

Aircrack is a wireless hacking tool for auditing wireless networks. It can be used as a sniffer and a WEP/WPA key cracker, as shown in Figure 1-5. Aircrack can recover 40-bit and 104-bit WEP keys after a large number of encrypted packets have been gathered.

Aircrack contains the following tools:

- *Airodump*: An 802.11 packet capture program
- *Aireplay*: An 802.11 packet injection program
- *Aircrack*: A tool that finds static WEP and WPA-PSK keys
- *Airdecap*: A tool that decrypts WEP/WPA capture files

Step 6: Spoof a MAC Address

The ***media access control (MAC) address*** is a unique address that is specific to a system. Generally, a MAC address can be spoofed with very little effort. Access control lists (ACLs) hold a list of MAC addresses that are unique to a system and that enable network transmission. The MAC address ACLs are not secured and can be accessed by an attacker who listens to a wireless network transmission. An attacker can spoof a MAC address gained from an ACL and conduct MAC flooding attacks.

MAC flooding is a computer network enumeration and footprinting technique (attack) that involves the spoofing of a network interface's unique MAC address, as shown in Figure 1-6. The technique focuses on the limited ability of network switches to store MAC addresses and their corresponding physical port mappings internally.

Step 7: Jam the Signal

Jammers are devices used to block wireless network communication within a specific area. Jammers can be stealthily installed in offices, conference rooms, or restaurants to absorb network traffic and thus stop wireless

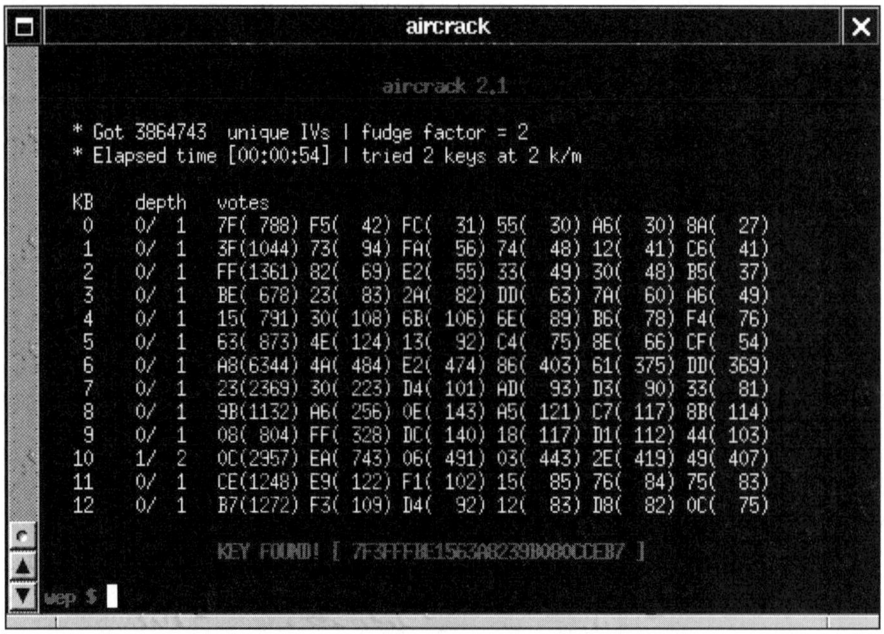

Figure 1-5 Aircrack can be used to brute-force encryption keys.

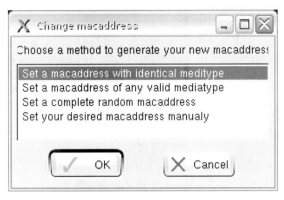

Figure 1-6 MAC flooding involves spoofing a network interface's MAC address.

network communication. This can also lead to a denial-of-service attack, wherein users of mobile devices cannot connect to the access point.

The following are some of the different types of jammers used to block signals:

- *Mobile phone jammer*: These are generally designed to block cell phone signals.
- *Video jammer*: This type of jammer blocks the communications of wireless video cameras.
- *Bluetooth jammer*: This devices blocks Bluetooth traffic.
- *Wi-Fi jammer*: This blocks wireless network traffic, such as the traffic on a wireless LAN (WLAN).

Step 8: Sniff the Wireless Traffic

A *sniffer* is a network protocol analyzer that identifies the type of protocol utilized, the IP, the server name, and the host associated with a packet. Sniffing the wireless traffic is done for the following reasons:

- Packet capturing
- Decoding the captured data and presenting it in a readable format
- Providing information about the type of protocol used
- Illegal activities such as stealing passwords or important financial data
- Capturing e-mail, attached files, and instant messages

Step 9: Attempt a Man-In-The-Middle Attack

A *man-in-the middle (MITM) attack* is an attack in which an attacker intercepts packets, reads or alters them, and then sends them on to their proper destination. MITM attacks can be either eavesdropping or manipulation attacks.

Eavesdropping

Eavesdropping does not require a physical medium. An attacker in the vicinity of the wireless network can receive traffic on the wireless network without any considerable effort or advanced technology. The entire data frame sent across the network can be examined in real time or stored for later assessment. In order to prevent hackers from acquiring sensitive information, several layers of encryption should be implemented. WEP is one type of encryption used on wireless networks. Unfortunately, WEP can be cracked with freely available tools on the net, but other protocols, such as WPA, have been developed as substitutes for WEP. However, many networks may still be using WEP.

Accessing e-mail using the POP or IMAP protocols is also risky, as these protocols are unencrypted. A determined hacker can potentially log gigabytes worth of WEP-protected traffic in an effort to postprocess the data and break the protection. This makes the wireless network more vulnerable to eavesdropping.

Manipulation

Manipulation occurs on a wireless link when an attacker is able to intercept the victim's encrypted data, manipulate it, and retransmit the changed data to the victim's intended recipient. The attacker can change e-mails, instant messages, or database transactions. Manipulation attacks also occur when an attacker intercepts packets with encrypted data and changes the destination address to forward the packets to a different destination on the Internet.

Step 10: Attempt Rapid Traffic Generation

In this step, the tester sniffs the wireless network to identify source and destination MAC addresses. These addresses are visible for each packet, even when the contents of the packets are encrypted with WEP. This helps the tester determine the hosts on the wireless network.

The tester can then use the Aireplay tool that comes with Aircrack (Figure 1-7). This tool has the ability to generate a large number of packets in a few minutes and crack WEP keys after gathering encrypted packets on the network.

Step 11: Try to Inject an Encrypted Packet

WEPWedgie is a tool that permits a user to craft custom packets, as shown in Figure 1-8. The tool listens to traffic on the network and watches for authentication traffic. It then captures data in that traffic to acquire the WEP keys. Once these keys have been captured, the user can craft the custom packets and send them over the network, using the correct WEP key. A tester can use this tool to inject custom encrypted packets on a wireless network. This allows the tester to test the network's vulnerability to certain packet injection attacks.

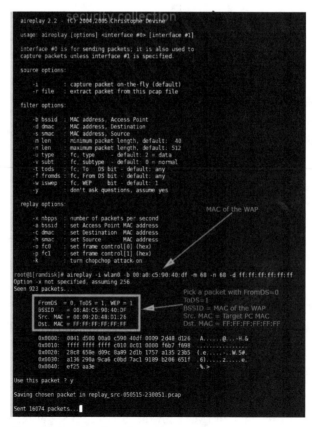

Figure 1-7   Aireplay allows the user to generate a large number of packets in a short amount of time.

```
witiwsl / # prgasnarf -c 1
Auth Frame:  Auth Type: Shared-Key - 00 01:00:01:00
Auth Frame:  Auth Type: Shared-Key - 01 01:00:02:00 :seq = 02 : Challenge Frame?
Auth Frame:  [3]Encrypted Auth Response
Auth Frame:  [4]responder OK with auth

BSSID: 0023ef3f202f    SourceMAC: 0060c10bb76e
Created 136byte PRGA for IV: b9:00:95
Created prgafile.dat in current directory
witiwsl / # wepwedgie -h c0:a8:00:be -t c0:a8:00:01 -S 2 -c 1
Pingscanning Selected
Reading prgafile.dat
BSSID:      00:23:ef:3f:20:2f
Source MAC: 00:60:c1:0b:b7:6e
IV:         b9:00:95:00
Pingscan
Setting last byte of target IP to 0 -- scanning 192.168.0.0-192.168.0.255
Injecting Ping....192.168.0.190->192.168.0.0
Injecting Ping....192.168.0.190->192.168.0.1
Injecting Ping....192.168.0.190->192.168.0.2
Injecting Ping....192.168.0.190->192.168.0.3
Injecting Ping....192.168.0.190->192.168.0.4
Injecting Ping    192 168 0 190->192 168 0 5
```

Figure 1-8   Packet injection attacks can be run with WEPWedgie.

```
witiwsl / # tethereal -nr test.pcap
  1   0.000000 00:60:c1:0b:b7:6e -> 00:10:5a:35:8e:c1 IEEE 802.11 Data
witiwsl / # switch-to-wlanng
witiwsl / # monitor.wlan wlan0 1
witiwsl / # time -p chopchop -burst 40 -m 00:60:c1:0b:b7:6e \
  -b 00:23:ef:3f:20:2f -p test.pcap
00:60:c1:0b:b7:6e 6
00:23:ef:3f:20:2f 6
0
first pass
-------------------
packet number 001
 OK

second pass
real 34.35
user 0.01
sys 9.30
witiwsl / # tethereal -nr test.pcap.dec
  1   0.000000 192.168.0.192 -> 192.168.0.2  ICMP Echo (ping) request
```

Figure 1-9   Chopchop allows a user to decrypt a packet without the WEP key.

Step 12: Attempt Single-Packet Decryption

Chopchop is a tool that allows a user to decrypt a single packet without having the WEP key, as shown in Figure 1-9. This tool replays an individual encrypted packet after modifying a single byte. It then sends the packet to the WAP (wireless access point) to see if it is accepted. By evaluating the WAP's response to each altered packet, Chopchop is able to find the plaintext value of each byte and decrypt the entire packet.

Step 13: Document Everything

As steps are taken to test a wireless network, the tester should document every step to ensure a high quality of testing and to avoid liability.

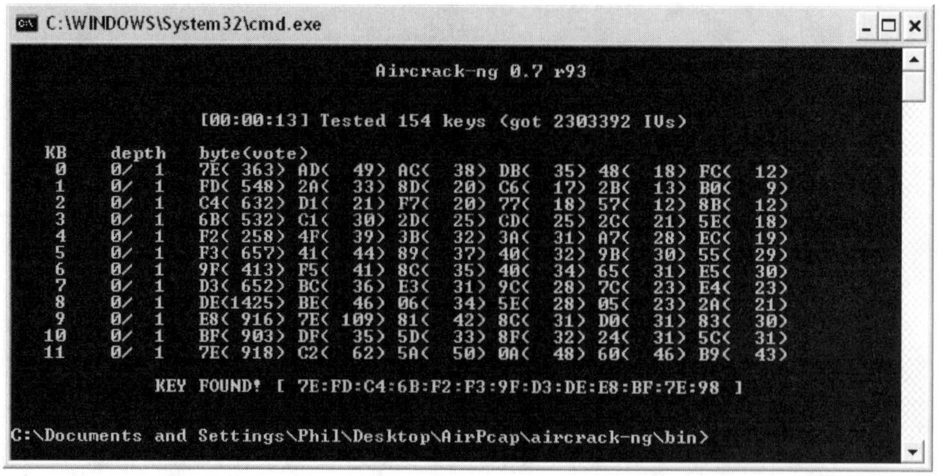

Figure 1-10   The Aircrack-ng suite can be used to crack WEP keys.

Wireless Penetration Testing Tools

Aircrack-ng

Aircrack-ng is a set of tools for auditing wireless networks. It includes the following programs:

- *Airodump*: 802.11 packet capture program
- *Aireplay*: 802.11 packet injection program
- *Aircrack*: Static WEP and WPA-PSK key cracker
- *Airdecap*: Decrypts WEP/WPA capture files

The Aircrack-ng suite (Figure 1-10) determines WEP keys using two methods. The first method is via the PTW approach (Pyshkin, Tews, and Weinmann). The main advantage of the PTW approach is that very few data packets are required to crack the WEP key.

The second method is the FMS/KoreK method. The FMS/KoreK method incorporates various statistical attacks to discover the WEP key and uses these in combination with brute forcing.

KisMAC

KisMAC (Figure 1-11) is a free stumbler application for Mac OS X that puts the computer's wireless card into monitor mode. It has the ability to run completely invisibly and send no probe requests.

NetStumbler

NetStumbler (Figure 1-12) is a tool for Windows that facilitates the detection of wireless LANs using the 802.11b, 802.11a, and 802.11g WLAN standards. NetStumbler can be used for the following applications:

- Wardriving
- Verifying network configurations
- Finding locations with poor coverage in a WLAN
- Detecting causes of wireless interference
- Detecting rogue access points
- Aiming directional antennas for long-haul WLAN links

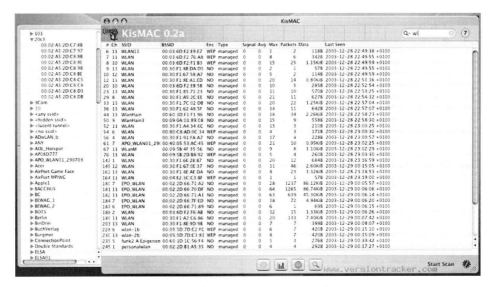

Figure 1-11   KisMAC is a tool used to put wireless cards into monitor mode.

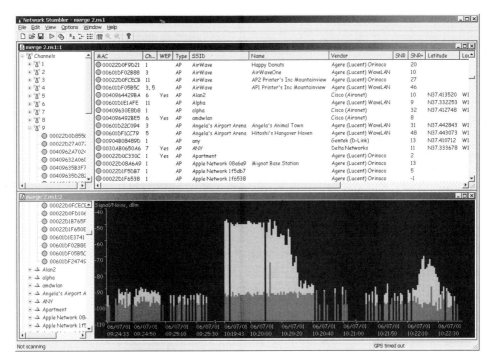

Figure 1-12   NetStumbler allows a user to find hidden wireless networks.

Kismet

Kismet (Figure 1-13) is an 802.11 layer-2 wireless network detector, sniffer, and intrusion detection system. Kismet will work with any wireless card that supports raw monitoring mode and can sniff 802.11b, 802.11a, and 802.11g traffic.

Kismet identifies networks by passively collecting packets, detecting standard named networks, detecting (and given time, decloaking) hidden networks, and inferring the presence of nonbeaconing networks via data traffic.

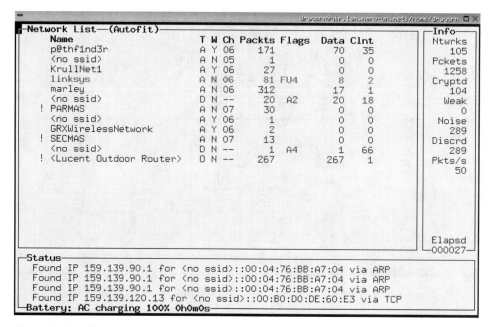

Figure 1-13 Kismet can detect wireless networks and function as an intrusion detection system.

Kismet includes the following features:

- Ethereal/Tcpdump-compatible data logging
- AirSnort-compatible weak-IV packet logging
- Network IP range detection
- Built-in channel hopping and multicard split channel hopping
- Hidden network SSID decloaking
- Graphical mapping of networks
- Client/server architecture allows multiple clients to view a single Kismet server simultaneously
- Manufacturer and model identification of access points and clients
- Detection of known default access point configurations
- Runtime decoding of WEP packets for known networks
- Named pipe output for integration with other tools, such as a layer-3 IDS like Snort
- Multiplexing of multiple simultaneous capture sources on a single Kismet instance
- Distributed remote drone sniffing

AirSnort

AirSnort (Figure 1-14) is a wireless LAN (WLAN) tool that recovers encryption keys. It operates by passively monitoring transmissions and computing the encryption key when enough packets have been gathered. It requires approximately 5–10 million encrypted packets to be gathered. Once enough packets have been gathered, AirSnort can guess the encryption password within a second.

Ethereal

Network professionals around the world use Ethereal (Figure 1-15) for troubleshooting, analysis, software development, protocol development, and education. Its open-source license allows talented experts in the networking community to add enhancements.

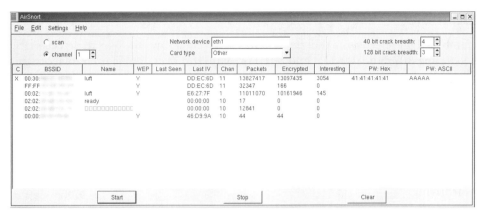

Figure 1-14   AirSnort can be used to recover wireless encryption keys.

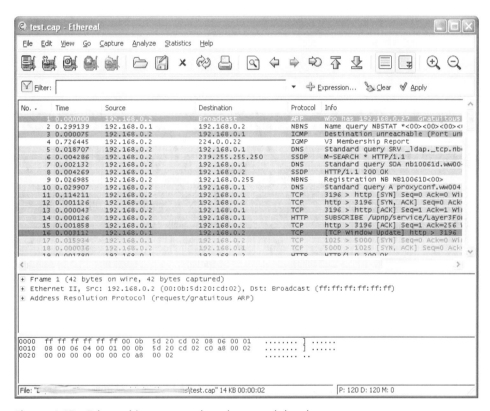

Figure 1-15   Ethereal is a protocol analyzer and developer.

WEPCrack

WEPCrack (Figure 1-16) is an open-source tool for breaking 802.11 WEP secret keys. It is useful for capturing SSIDs, AP MAC addresses, or authentication data. The current tools are Perl-based and include the following scripts:

- *WeakIVGen.pl*: This script allows a simple emulation of IV/encrypted output that can often be observed with a WEP-enabled 802.11 access point. The script generates IV combinations that can weaken the secret key used to encrypt the WEP traffic.

- *prism-getIV.pl*: This script relies on output from Prismdump (or from Ethereal captures) and looks for IVs that match the pattern known to weaken secret keys. This script also captures the first byte of the encrypted output and places it and the weak IVs in a log file.

- *WEPCrack.pl*: This script uses data collected or generated by WeakIVGen to attempt to determine the secret key. It works with either 40-bit or 128-bit WEP.

MiniStumbler

MiniStumbler (Figure 1-17) is a tool for Windows CE that allows the user to detect wireless local area networks (WLANs) using 802.11b, 802.11a, and 802.11g. MiniStumbler can be used to accomplish the following goals:

- Verify that a network is set up as intended.
- Find locations with poor coverage in a WLAN.
- Detect other networks that may be causing interference on a network.
- Detect rogue access points in a workplace.
- Help to aim directional antennas for long-haul WLAN links.
- Wardriving.

AirMagnet

AirMagnet (Figure 1-18) allows the user to mitigate all types of wireless threats, enforce enterprise policies, prevent performance problems and audit the regulatory compliance of Wi-Fi assets.

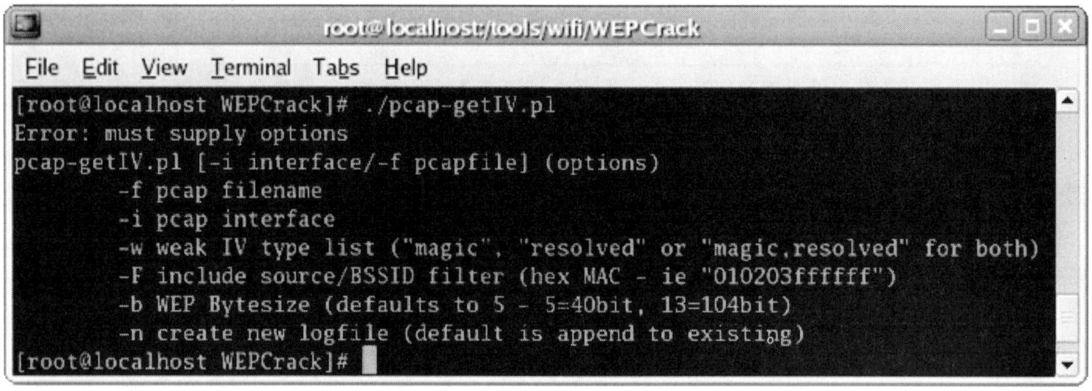

root@localhost:/tools/wifi/WEPCrack
File Edit View Terminal Tabs Help
[root@localhost WEPCrack]# ./pcap-getIV.pl
Error: must supply options
pcap-getIV.pl [-i interface/-f pcapfile] (options)
-f pcap filename
-i pcap interface
-w weak IV type list ("magic", "resolved" or "magic,resolved" for both)
-F include source/BSSID filter (hex MAC - ie "010203ffffff")
-b WEP Bytesize (defaults to 5 - 5=40bit, 13=104bit)
-n create new logfile (default is append to existing)
[root@localhost WEPCrack]#

Figure 1-16 WEPCrack can be used to crack WEP keys.

MiniStumbler 12:09
MAC Chan SSID SNR
0090D100BF6C 11 WLAN 5
0090D100B93B 11 WLAN
0090D100CC6F 11+ WLAN 10
0090D100BEC5 6 WLAN
004033AFC3D1 10 Wireless
0090D100CAA5 11 WLAN 17
0090D100BE02 1 WLAN
Ready 3 APs GPS Off 7/7
File View Options

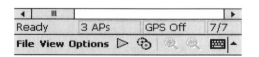

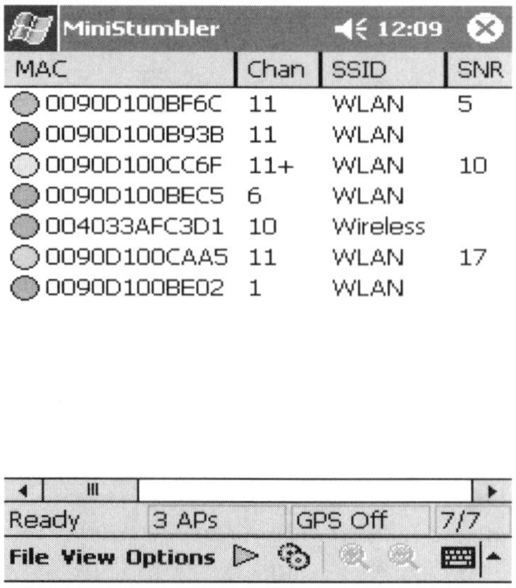

Figure 1-17 MiniStumbler can be used to detect hidden WLANs.

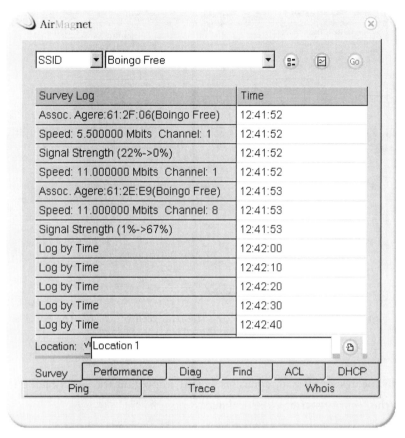

Figure 1-18 AirMagnet is a wireless monitoring tool.

AirMagnet includes the following features:

- Automatically defends against threats
- Maximizes uptime
- Simplifies investigation and workflow
- Creates and enforces policies
- Reviews security policy compliance and WLAN vulnerabilities
- Blocks rogue access points and ad hoc devices

WirelessMon

WirelessMon (Figure 1-19) is a software tool that allows users to monitor the status of wireless Wi-Fi adapter(s) and gather information about nearby wireless access points and hot spots in real time. It can log the information collected into a file, provide comprehensive graphing of signal levels, and provide real-time IP and 802.11 Wi-Fi statistics.

WirelessMon includes the following features:

- Verifies that 802.11 network configuration is correct
- Checks signal levels from local Wi-Fi and nearby networks
- Creates signal strength maps of an area
- Has GPS support for logging and mapping signal strength
- Helps to locate sources of interference for a network
- Scans for hot spots in a localized area (wardriving)

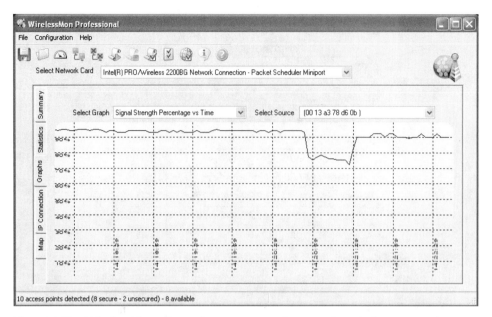

Figure 1-19 WirelessMon allows the user to monitor nearby wireless networks.

- Correctly locates wireless antennas (especially important for directional antennas)
- Verifies the security settings for local access points
- Measures network speed and throughput, and displays available data rates

Chapter Summary

- Wireless monitoring is a passive approach to testing wireless networks that allows an administrator to determine if a network has any obvious security flaws.
- WEP uses shared secret keys of 40 or 104 bits to encrypt and decrypt data.
- MAC address ACLs are not secured and can be accessed by an attacker who listens in on a wireless network transmission.
- An attacker in the vicinity of a wireless network can intercept traffic on the wireless network without any considerable effort or advanced technology.
- By evaluating the WAP's response to each altered packet it sends, Chopchop is able to find the plaintext value of each byte and decrypt the entire packet.
- As steps are taken to test a wireless network, the tester should document every step to ensure a high quality of testing and to avoid liability.

## Chapter 2

Advanced Wireless Testing

Objectives

After completing this chapter, you should be able to:

- Understand wireless standards and terminology
- Understand wireless technologies
- Understand wireless encryption
- Understand wireless attacks
- Wardrive with NetStumbler
- Understand how NetStumbler works
- Conduct active and passive WLAN detection
- Disable a beacon
- Run NetStumbler
- Conduct wireless penetration testing with Windows
- Use aircrack-ng
- Crack WEP encryption

Key Terms

Access points (APs)   hardware devices or software used to connect wireless users to a wired network for communication

Bluetooth   a short-range wireless technology that operates at 2.4 to 2.485 GHz

Channel   a certain frequency within a given frequency band

Chipset   a group of circuits or microchips designed to work together

Narrowband   the transmission and reception of data at a narrow frequency band

Remote Authentication Dial-In User Service (RADIUS)   a protocol used for centralized authentication, authorization, and accounting during network access by a wireless device

Service set ID (SSID)   the sequence of characters that is attached to each packet sent over a wireless network and is used to identify that network

Social engineering   the process of manipulating people into divulging confidential information that they might not give out under normal circumstances

Wardriving   the act of moving around a specific area and mapping the population of wireless access points

Introduction to Advanced Wireless Testing

Wireless refers to any electrical or electronics operation that is carried out without the use of a wire. Wireless communication allows networks to extend to places that might otherwise be unreachable by wired networks. Wireless, by its very nature, has no well-defined perimeter, making security more challenging. The following sections describe terms that are essential to any discussion of wireless testing.

Wireless Terminology

Access Points

Access points (APs) are the hardware devices or software used to connect wireless users to a wired network for communication. APs act as bridges or hubs between wired LANs and wireless networks. APs are necessary for providing strong wireless security and are also used for increasing the physical range of the services that wireless users access. The range of APs can be increased with repeaters, which amplify the network's radio signals.

Channels

A *channel* is a certain frequency within a given frequency band. It is necessary for a wireless client and an AP to communicate over the same channel. For example, the 802.11b standard works within the 2.4- to 2.4835-GHz range. Channel 1 is 2.401 GHz, channel 2 is 2.402 GHz, channel 3 is 2.4.03 GHz, and so on. The 2.4 GHz band has a total of 80 channels. When a station initializes or moves from one AP to another, it will tune to the channel of another AP. The client will tune to the strongest signal available because it believes that is the closest AP. When using several APs, they all need to be set to different channels to ensure that signals do not interfere with each other.

Service Set ID (SSID)

A *service set ID (SSID)* is the sequence of characters that is attached to each packet sent over a wireless network and is used to identify that network, as shown in Figure 2-1. This is useful for identifying packets on a particular network when there are a number of networks present. The SSID can contain a maximum of 32 alphanumeric

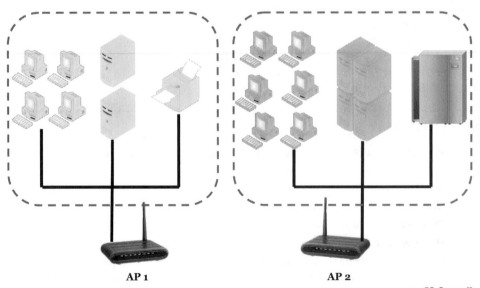

AP 1   AP 2

Figure 2-1   Service set IDs (SSIDs) are used to differentiate packets between networks.

characters. All wireless devices that communicate with each other have the same SSID. The SSID is used to uniquely identify a set of wireless network devices in the given service set. There are two main variants of SSID:

1. *IBSS (independent basic service set)*: A service set in which wireless devices communicate with each other directly; there is no use of access points

2. *ESS (extended service set)*: A service set in which a number of BSSs are joined using access points

Any hosts that wish to participate in a particular WLAN must be configured with the proper SSID, and various hosts can be segmented into different WLANs by using different SSIDs. The reasons for segmenting different wireless devices are the same reasons for segmenting wired systems on a network; they require access to different resources, they are used for different business functions, and they have different levels of trust.

The SSID may be provided when a host attempts to join a WLAN, or it may be advertised by sending out beacons from the AP to any listening hosts. For a WLAN to be 802.11b compliant, the AP will broadcast SSIDs, and this is the default configuration. The SSID should not be seen as a reliable security mechanism, since it is not secured and is easily accessible. A host only needs to eavesdrop on wireless transmissions from a specific AP to learn the SSID being used.

Vendors have SSIDs set to default values that most companies do not change, so attackers can easily guess them, even if they are not broadcast. For example, most Cisco APs use *tsunami* as the default SSID. An AP can be configured to broadcast its SSID, which means that hosts do not need to know the SSID beforehand. If this configuration is turned off, then the host must have the same SSID as the AP, which provides a better degree of security.

The following are some of the default SSIDs different vendors use:

- *Cisco:* "tsunami"
- *3Com:* "101"
- *Lucent/Cabletron:* "RoamAbout Default Network Name"
- *Baystack 650/660:* "Default SSID"
- *Compaq:* "Compaq"
- *Addtron, D-Link, SMC:* "WLAN"
- *Intel:* "intel"
- *Linksys:* "linksys" or "Wireless"
- *SOHOware NetBlaster II:* "MAC Address!!!"

Chipsets

A *chipset* is simply a group of circuits or microchips designed to work together. Chipsets are generally used for motherboard chips or the chips used on expansion cards. The following chipsets are important for wireless applications:

- *Prism II chipsets:* These chipsets have the following features:
  - Well supported in most wireless applications
  - Fully compatible with 802.11
  - Include a 2.4-GHz direct sequence modem
  - Include features like roaming and WEP
- *Orinoco chipsets:* These chipsets have the following features:
  - Can usually be determined by small N-post adapter on the end of the chipset
  - Used by Lucent, Avaya, and Enterasys
- *Cisco chipsets:* These chipsets have the following features:
  - Usually supported by applications
  - 2.4GHz/802.11b wireless standard
  - Indoor range of 130 feet at 11 Mbps, 350 feet at 1 Mbps
  - Up to 128-bit WEP encryption

- *Atheros chipsets:* These chipsets have the following features:
  - Extend the range and reduce the power consumption of 802.11 wireless networks
  - Combine a wireless system with high-performance radio frequency (RF), which provides highly integrated chipsets
  - Combine single and digital semiconductor designs

Wireless Standards

When most people say *wireless* these days, they are referring to one of the 802.11 standards. There are four main 802.11 standards: a, b, g, and n. 802.11 has weak authentication and encryption mechanisms.

802.11 Types

The 802.11 standards are a set of standards for WLAN. They denote an over-the-air interface between a wireless client and a base station or access point. The following are some of the different flavors of 802.11:

- *802.11 Legacy*: 802.11 Legacy standards include the following basic features:
  - 2 Mbps theoretical
  - Uses CSMA/CA for collision detection and avoidance
  - Can use either FHSS or DSSS for modulation
- *802.11b*: 802.11b standards include the following basic features:
  - Operates at 20 MHz, in the 2.4-GHz range
  - Most widely used and accepted form of wireless networking
  - Theoretical speeds of up to 11 Mbps
  - Actual speeds of up to 5.9 Mbps when TCP (Transmission Control Protocol) is used (error checking)
  - Actual speeds of up to 7.1 Mbps when UDP (User Datagram Protocol) is used (no error checking)
  - Uses DSSS modulation, splitting the 2.4-GHz band into channels
  - SSID (service set identifier) used for network differentiation
  - Can transmit up to 8 km in the city
  - Not as easily immersed as an 802.11a signal
  - Can cause or receive interference from microwave ovens (microwaves in general), wireless telephones, and other wireless appliances operating at the same frequency
- *802.11a*: 802.11a standards include the following basic features:
  - Works at 40 MHz, in the 5-GHz range
  - Theoretical transfer rates of up to 54 Mbps
  - Actual transfer rates of about 26.4 Mbps
  - Use is limited, as it is almost a line-of-sight transmittal that requires multiple WAPs (wireless access points)
  - It uses a modulation technique called coded orthogonal frequency division multiplexing (COFDM)
  - Immersed more easily than other wireless implementations
  - Overcame the challenge of indoor radio frequency
  - Uses a single-carrier, delay-spread system
  - Not backward compatible with 802.11b
  - Not widely deployed
- *802.11g*: 802.11g standards include the following basic features:
  - Operates at the same frequency range as 802.11b
  - Theoretical throughput of 54 Mbps
  - Several factors responsible for actual transmission rate, but average rate is 24.7 Mbps

	802.11	802.11a	802.11b	802.11g	802.11n
Frequency	2.4GHz	5GHz	2.4GHz	2.4GHz	2.4 or 5GHz
Theoretical Rate(s)	2 Mbps theoretical	6, 9, 12, 18, 24, 36, 48, 54 Mbps	1, 2, 5.5, or 11 Mbps	6, 9, 12, 18, 24, 36, 48, 54 Mbps	600 Mbps
Modulation	FHSS/DSSS	COFDM	DSSS	OFDM	DSSS, CCK, and OFDM
Effective Data Throughput	1.2 Mbps	Actual transfer rates of about 26.4 Mbps	5.9 Mbps (TCP) and 7.1 Mbps (UDP)	Average rate is 24.7 Mbps	100-200 Mbps
Advertised Range	300 ft	225 ft	300 ft	300 ft	600 ft
Encryption	Yes	Yes	Yes	Yes	Yes
Encryption Type	40-bit RC4	40- or 104-bit RC4	40- or 104-bit RC4	40- or 104-bit RC4	40- or 104-bit RC4
Authentication	No	No	No	No	Yes
Network Support	Ethernet	Ethernet	Ethernet	Ethernet	WLAN

Figure 2-2   The 802.11 standard has variations that each have specific capabilities.

- Is backward compatible with 802.11b wireless networks
- Natively uses OFDM
- *802.11n*: 802.11n standards include the following basic features:
  - Based on multiple-input/multiple-output (MIMO) technology; MIMO uses a radio-wave phenomenon called multipath, which transfers the information to a receiving antenna multiple times by different routes and at different times
  - Doubles the data rate by increasing the channel width from 20 MHz to 40 MHz
  - Increased data rate up to 600 Mbps
  - Works at RF band 2.4 GHz or 5 GHz
  - Natively uses DSSS, CCK, and OFDM modulation
  - Has effective data throughput from 100 to 200 Mbps
  - Has reduced interframe spacing (RIFS), which improves efficiency

Figure 2-2 illustrates the differences between the variations in the 802.11 standard.

Core Issues with 802.11

The following issues make the 802.11 standards vulnerable:

- *Perimeter security:* A wired network runs from point A to point B, while a wireless network runs as far as the wireless signals can reach through the air. Because of this, eavesdropping and packet sniffing are easy to accomplish. For this reason, many government facilities cannot use wireless, even with higher-layer encryption. Perimeter security is sometimes implemented by disabling SSID broadcasts; however, these stealthed networks are still vulnerable.

- *Performance:*
  - RF communications are easy to take down.
  - The AP with the strongest signal wins.

- With CSMA/CA, performance is crippled. With the addition of WEP, performance drops even further.
- *Vulnerability to certain attacks:*
  - Easy access to the local segment means easy DoS attacks at the network level.
  - Packet flooding and ARP spoofing are also comparatively easy to initiate.

Other Types of Wireless

HiperLAN2

HiperLAN2 is the European WLAN standard. It has a range of 5 GHz and a data rate of 54 Mbps. HiperLAN2 allows for the interconnecting of any type of fixed network technology and provides separate Quality of Service (QoS) for separate connections. QoS support enables the user to separate mixed information such as voice and video. HiperLAN offers unicast, multicast, and broadcast transmissions.

Bluetooth

Bluetooth is short-range wireless technology that operates at 2.4 to 2.485 GHz. It uses a spread spectrum, frequency hopping, full-duplex signal at a nominal rate of 1,600 hops/sec. The maximum data transmission rate for Bluetooth ranges between 721 kbps and 10 Mbps, depending on the version. It is able to handle both data and voice transmissions simultaneously.

802.16—Wireless Metropolitan Area Network (WMAN)

The IEEE 802.16 group is a broadband wireless access group that provides standards for WMAN. It addresses the "first mile/last mile" connection in WMAN. It supports the use of bandwidth between 10 and 66 GHz, and describes a media access control (MAC) layer. It allows for interoperability between devices.

This standard supports the progress of fixed broadband wireless access systems to permit rapid worldwide operation of innovative, cost-effective, and interoperable multivendor broadband wireless access products.

Infrared (IR)

Because IR works at a frequency just under visible light, it cannot successfully penetrate physical objects like walls, ceilings, floors, desks, etc.; thus, it is restricted to short-range implementations and must be in sight of its target.

Narrowband

Narrowband describes the transmission and reception of data at a narrow frequency band. This term describes the specific frequency range set by the FCC. It sets the range for radio services including a paging system from 50 cps to 64 kbps.

Spread Spectrum

Spread spectrum provides a more reliable signal and throughput than narrowband. Spread spectrum also allows unrelated products to share the same spectrum with minimal interference. Figure 2-3 shows the difference between spread spectrum, narrowband, and infrared.

Spread spectrum communications are data signals that are spread across a wider frequency bandwidth of the radio channel. This means that a set of radio frequencies is used and the data is spread across them. An analogy could be a water hose; the user can only get so much water through a water hose because it only has one channel available to it. A fire hose has more channels involved; thus, more water can be delivered at a faster rate.

It uses two different methods:

1. *Frequency-hopping spread spectrum (FHSS)*: Most signals use the digital technique known as frequency hopping. The signal is broadcast over a number of radio frequencies.
2. *Direct-sequence spread spectrum (DSSS)*: In the transmitted signal, each bit is represented by multiple bits.

DSSS versus FHSS Interference is a major issue in wireless transmissions because it can corrupt signals as they travel. Other devices working in the same frequency space can cause interference. The FHSS approach to this is to hop between different frequencies so that if another device is operating at the same frequency, the signal will not be drastically affected.

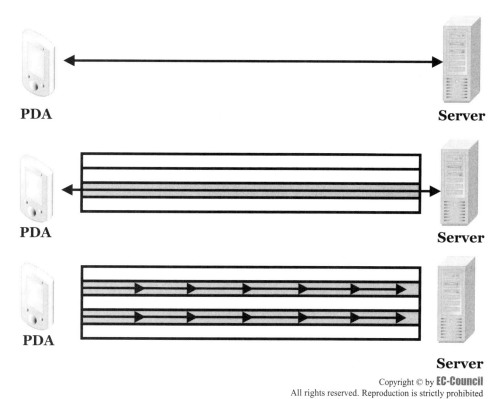

Figure 2-3 Spread spectrum uses multiple channels to communicate.

DSSS takes a different approach by adding sub-bits to a packet. The sub-bits are used at the receiving end to reassemble the message. The sub-bits provide error recovery instructions also, just like parity does in RAID implementations. The sub-bits are called a chip and the way the chip is applied to a message is called the chipping code.

If a signal using FHSS is corrupted, it has to be re-sent. However, by using DSSS, even if the message is a bit distorted, the signal can still be regenerated. For the receiver to be able to properly receive data using DSSS, it has to know how to interpret the sub-bits. This is known as "unspreading the chip."

Wi-Fi Equipment

A typical wireless infrastructure comprises devices that connect to the network. These devices include antennas, access points, mobile stations, base station subsystems, network subsystems, a base station controller, a terminal, a mobile switching center, a wireless modem, and a wireless router.

Antennas

Antennas are important for sending and receiving radio waves. They convert electrical impulses into radio waves and vice versa. The following types of antennas are commonly used:

- *Directional antennas:* These antennas concentrate radio signals in a particular direction.

- *Omnidirectional antennas:* These antennas radiate or receive equally in all directions.

- *Aperture antennas:* These antennas have a physical opening through which the propagation of electromagnetic waves takes place. These types of antennas are developed from waveguide technology.

- *Leaky wave antennas:* These antennas obtain millimeter waves using dielectric guides, microstrip lines, coplanar lines, and slot lines.

- *Reflector antennas:* Reflector antennas are used to concentrate electromagnetic energy that is radiated or received at a focal point. These reflectors are generally parabolic.

- *Monopole antennas:* These are simple antennas that are omnidirectional (in azimuth) and if, they are half a wavelength long, have a gain of 2.15 dBi in the horizontal plane. They are half a dipole placed in half space, with a perfectly conducting, infinite surface at the boundary.

- *Dipole antennas:* In this antenna, two wires are oriented horizontally or vertically and pointed in opposite directions. One end of the wire is connected to a radio, while the other is suspended in free space.
- *Yagi antennas:* Yagi antennas or aerials are the most directive antennas. They are generally used where gain and directivity are required. A dipole is the main radiating element.
- *Log-periodic antennas:* Many other antennas have comparatively narrow bandwidth, but log-periodic antennas provide gain and directivity over a large bandwidth. They consist of a number of dipole elements.
- *Active antennas:* Active antennas consist of small whip antennas that supply incoming RF to a pre-amplifier, whose output is then connected to the antenna input of the receiver. These antennas are designed for receiving purposes.

Access Points

An access point is a piece of wireless communication hardware that creates a central point of wireless connectivity. Similar to a hub, the access point is a common connection point for devices in a wireless network.

PC Cards

PC cards are credit card–size peripherals that add memory, mass storage, and I/O capabilities to computers in a rugged and compact form.

Wireless Cards

The wireless network card locates and communicates with the access point to give users network access.

Wireless Modems

Wireless modems are devices that are used to connect computers to a WLAN without using cable wiring. It is a modem that is connected to a wireless network instead of a telephone system.

Wireless Routers

A wireless router is a simple router with a wireless interface. It is a device that connects wireless networks.

Wireless Gateways

Wireless gateways include the following:

- Wireless media gateway
- Wireless VoIP gateway
- Wireless presentation gateway
- Hot-spot gateway

Vulnerabilities to 802.1x and RADIUS

The *Remote Authentication Dial-In User Service (RADIUS)* protocol is used for centralized authentication, authorization, and accounting during network access by a wireless device. Virtual private network (VPN) servers, wireless access points, authenticating Ethernet switches, digital subscriber line (DSL) access, and other network access types support RADIUS. Network managers can minimize the risks associated with information distribution across devices by using RADIUS. Authentication and permission attributes can be integrated into a single server.

RADIUS does not deal with the encryption of data. When a user wants access to the network, secure files, or network locations for the first time, the user must input a name and password and submit those over the network to the RADIUS server. The server then verifies that the individual has an account and if so, ensures that the person uses the correct password before the network can be accessed.

Some early 802.1x implementations cannot use the per-session keys outlined in the IEEE 802.1x standard to encrypt the data. Such implementations are weak against a number of WEP attacks. No means of authenticating the access point is available to the user. An attacker can easily spoof an access point and forward a user's credentials to the RADIUS server.

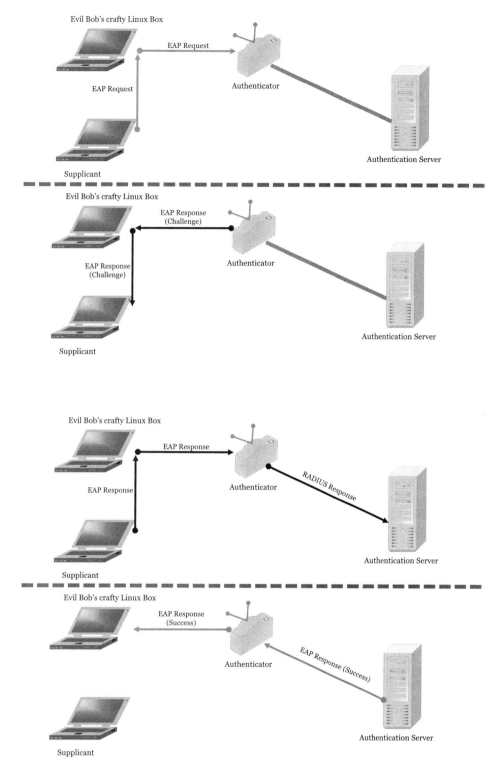

Figure 2-4   RADIUS can allow attackers to gain a user's credentials. (*Continues*)

If the RADIUS server is used for authentication methods other than EAP, then the following vulnerabilities can apply, as shown in Figure 2-4:

- The RADIUS shared secret is vulnerable to an offline dictionary attack, based on the capture of the response authenticator or message-authenticator attribute. Changing the shared secret between authentication methods will fix this vulnerability.

- RADIUS can be vulnerable to a brute-force attack.

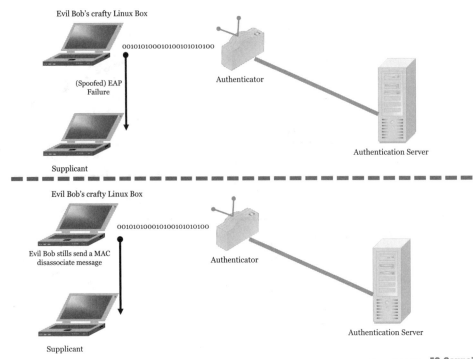

Figure 2-4 RADIUS can allow attackers to gain a user's credentials. (*Continued*)

Encryption Standards

Wired Equivalent Privacy (WEP)

Wired Equivalent Privacy (WEP) is an optional encryption standard used in 802.11. In 802.11, it is executed in the MAC layer and is implemented by the network interface card (NIC) and the access point.

In a WLAN, when WEP is active, each packet is encrypted by taking the XOR of the original packet with the RC4 stream cipher. These packets are created using 64-bit keys. These keys consist of a 24-bit initialization vector (IV) and 40-bit WEP keys. An additional 4-byte integrity check value (ICV) is calculated and appended to the end of the original packet. This ICV also gets encrypted with the RC4 stream cipher. WEP that uses 128-bit keys to encrypt the data is known as WEP2.

WEP provides the following features:

- *Confidentiality:* It prevents link-layer eavesdropping.

- *Access control:* It restricts access to authorized persons.

- *Data integrity:* It protects data from being modified by a third party.

Encryption Process

When a message is to be encrypted, it is first passed through a CRC function, which is an error detection mechanism, and a CRC value is derived and attached to the message. When the receiving system receives this message, it performs the same CRC function and compares the two values. If the values are the same, the sending system can be assured that the message has not been modified.

Once the sending system attaches the CRC value, it then inserts the 24-bit IV into the RC4 algorithm, along with a 40-bit or 104-bit key to create a pseudorandom keystream. This keystream and plaintext data is then XORed bit-wise to create the encrypted message known as the ciphertext. It is this ciphertext that is then sent to the receiver, who performs the same actions in reverse to decrypt the message, as shown in Figure 2-5.

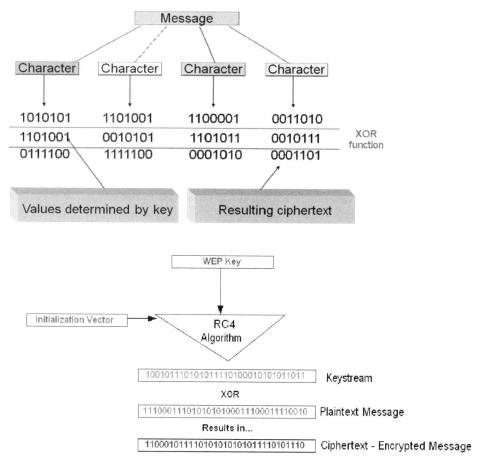

Figure 2-5 The WEP encryption process uses an RC4 algorithm to encode and decode the data content of a message.

All stream encryption algorithms generate a keystream that is used in its encryption and decryption process. It is important that the keystream be random and not easily guessed by potential attackers.

When WEP is implemented, it does not encrypt the entire transmission, only the data payload of the transmission. One of the main components of the encryption process, the IV, is sent in the clear so that the receiving station can use it in the decryption process. The IV is a random number that can be up to 24 bits long. The sole purpose of the IV is to make the keystream more random, instead of just using a key.

The goal of the attacker is to learn the different keystreams that a network uses, and the goal of the wireless device owner is to create a wide range of keystreams that are difficult to guess and that provide no patterns.

Chipping Sequence

A chipping sequence is used to encode signal data. All users in wireless broadband channels use the same frequency but have a different chipping sequence. It is like the mask that encodes the original signal, as shown in Figure 2-6.

Authentication Phase

In open system authentication (OSA), all transactions are clear, so an intruder can sniff the traffic and walk through the same steps to be authenticated and associated with an AP.

Shared-key authentication (SKA) encrypts most, but not all, encryption components for the authentication process and data transfers. This uses WEP encryption, which can easily be defeated.

The access criteria may include specific MAC addresses of hosts, but an intruder can easily change a MAC address to one that is on the list of accepted MAC addresses. When a wireless station wants to access a network, it sends a probe request packet on all channels so that any AP in range will respond.

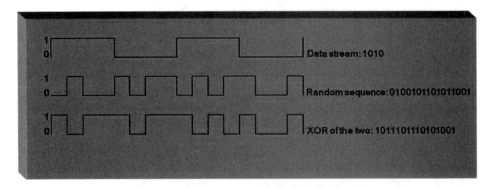

Figure 2-6   A chipping sequence is used to encode signal data.

The AP responds with packets containing the AP's SSID and other network information. When OSA is configured, the station will send an authentication request to the AP, and the AP will make an access decision based on its policy. When SKA is configured, the AP will send a challenge to the station, and the station encrypts it with its WEP key and sends it back to the AP. If the AP can successfully decrypt and obtain the challenge value, then the station has authorized access.

Association Phase

After the authentication phase, the station will send the AP an association request packet. If the AP has a policy to allow this station to access the network, it will associate the station to itself by placing the station in its association table. A wireless device has to be associated with an AP to access network resources, and not just be authenticated. The authentication and association phases authorize the device, and not the user. There is no way to know if an unauthorized user has stolen and is using an authorized device.

WEP Issues

WEP encryption has the following issues:

- RC32 is not sufficient to ensure complete cryptographic integrity of a packet. By capturing two packets, an attacker can reliably flip a bit in the encrypted stream and modify the checksum so that the packet is accepted.
- IVs are 24 bits. An AP broadcasting 1,500-byte packets at 11 Mbps would exhaust the entire IV space in 5 hours. This means that the IVs are repeated, and thus leaves WEP open to attack.
- *Known plaintext attacks:* When there is an IV collision, it becomes possible to reconstruct the RC4 keystream based off the IV and the decrypted payload of the packet.
- *Dictionary attacks:* WEP is based on a password. The small space of the initialization vector allows the attacker to create a decryption table.
- *Denial-of-service (DoS) attacks:* Associate and disassociate messages are not authenticated.
- Eventually, an attacker can construct a decryption table of reconstructed keystreams. With about 24 GB of space, an attacker can use this table to decrypt WEP packets in real time.
- A lack of centralized key management makes it difficult to change WEP keys with any regularity.
- The IV is a value that is used to randomize the keystream value, and each packet has an IV value. The standard only allows 24 bits, which can be used up within hours at a busy AP. Thus, IV values will be reused and vulnerable to attack.
- The standard does not dictate that each packet must have a unique IV, so vendors use only a small part of the available 24-bit possibilities. A mechanism that depends on randomness is not very random at all, and attackers can easily figure out the keystream and decrypt other messages.

Because most companies have configured their stations and APs to use the same shared key, or the default four keys, the randomness of the keystream relies heavily on the uniqueness of the IV value. The use of an IV and a key ensures that the keystream for each packet is different, but in most cases the IV changes while the key stays constant. Because there are only two main components to this encryption process when one stays constant, the randomization of the process decreases to an unacceptable level. A busy access point can use all available IV values (2^{24}) within hours, which requires the reuse of IV values. Repetition in a process that relies on randomness can end up in futile efforts and nonworthy results.

What makes the IV issue even worse is that the 802.11 standard does not require that each packet have a different IV value. In many implementations, the IV value only changes when the wireless NIC reinitializes, which is usually during a reboot. So, not only does 24 bits for the IV value not provide enough possible IV combination values, most implementations only use a handful of bits, thus not even using all that is available to them.

WEP Attacks

It takes at least 10,000 packets to discover a WEP key. A large amount of known data is the fastest way of determining as many keystreams as possible. WEPWedgie can be used to generate a large number of small packets.

Wi-Fi Protected Access (WPA)

WPA stands for Wi-Fi Protected Access. It is compatible with the 802.11i security standard. It is a software upgrade, but may also require a hardware upgrade.

WPA is a stopgap solution that exhibits the following features:

- It resolves WEP encryption issues. Its IVs are larger (48 bits instead of 24). Its shared key is utilized to negotiate and communicate temporal keys. Packets are encrypted using the temporal keys.

- It does not solve issues with the management frames.

- The collision avoidance mechanism can still be exploited.

- It is supported by most 802.11b hardware.

WPA2

WPA2 (Wi-Fi Protected Access 2) is compatible with the 802.11i standard. WPA2 supports most of the security features that are not supported by WPA. It provides stronger data protection and network access control.

WPA2 implements the National Institute of Standards and Technology (NIST) FIPS 140-2 compliant AES encryption algorithm and provides government-grade security.

WPA2 offers the following two modes of operation:

1. *WPA-Personal*: This version makes use of a setup password and protects against unauthorized network access.

2. *WPA-Enterprise*: This confirms the network user through a server.

Extensible Authentication Protocol (EAP)

Extensible Authentication Protocol (EAP) uses dynamic keys instead of the static WEP authentication key. The user's transmission must go through a WLAN AP to reach the server performing the authentication.

EAP allows the user to pass security authentication data between the RADIUS server, the AP, and the wireless user. It is a worldwide authentication framework frequently utilized in wireless networks and point-to-point connections. It can also be used in a wired network.

EAP supports the following authentication methods:

- Token cards and smart cards

- Kerberos

- One-time passwords

- Certificates

- Public-key authentication

Lightweight Extensible Authentication Protocol (LEAP)

The Lightweight Extensible Authentication Protocol (LEAP) is a proprietary, closed solution that offers username/password-based authentication between a wireless client and a RADIUS server.

LEAP conducts mutual authentication. It is used with the IEEE 802.1x standard for LAN port access control. LEAP includes the following features:

- It provides assurance to the client that the access point is authorized.
- It employs per-session keys that need to be changed regularly:
  - This makes the collection of a pad or weak IVs more difficult.
  - The secret key can be changed before the collection is complete.
- The user is authenticated, instead of the hardware, so MAC address access control lists are not needed.
- LEAP requires an authentication server (RADIUS) to support the access points.

TKIP (Temporal Key Integrity Protocol)

The Temporal Key Integrity Protocol (TKIP) is an element of the IEEE 802.11i encryption standard used in Wi-Fi Protected Access. TKIP eliminates the drawbacks of WEP by offering per-packet key mixing, a rekeying mechanism, and a message integrity check. It provides a guarantee that each data packet has been sent with its own encryption key.

The following points must be made about TKIP:

- Designed as a quick fix to overcome the reuse-of-encryption-key problem with WEP
- Still uses WEP RC4, but changes temporal key every 10,000 packets
- Mandates use of MIC to prevent packet forgery
- Secret key created during four-way handshake authentication
- Dynamically changes secret key
- Function used to create new keys based on the original secret key created during authentication
- IVs increased to 48 bits
- First 4 bits indicate QoS traffic class
- Remaining 44 bits are used as a counter
- More than 500 trillion keystreams possible
- IVs are hashed
- Harder to detect keystreams with the same IVs
- Uses existing device calculation capabilities to perform encryption operations
- Improves security, but is still only a short-term fix

TKIP combines the preshared key with the client's MAC and a larger IV to ensure that each client uses a different keystream.

Wireless Network Testing

The following tasks should be completed when conducting a wireless network test:

- Verify the distance at which wireless communications exceed the physical boundaries of the organization.
- Generate a list of devices needed/tried (antenna, card, amplifier, software, etc.).
- Verify authentication methods of the client devices.
- Verify that encryption is configured and running.
- Verify what key length is used.
- Verify the IP range of the network.
- Decide the level of physical access controls to access points and the equipment that controls them.
- Determine the protocols involved.
- Probe network for possible DoS problems.

- Review the access logs and check that no rogue devices can access the wireless network.
- Check that wireless network devices and other electronic devices do not interfere with each other at the same frequencies.
- Check that the access point will not enable the attacker to cause a DoS attack through an SNMP request.
- Check that the organization has an adequate security policy.
- Maintain a complete inventory of all wireless devices on the network.
- Determine if APs are turned off during portions of the day when they will not be in use.
- Verify that the AP SSIDs have been changed from the defaults.
- Verify that all wireless clients adhere to the following requirements:
  - Have antivirus software and a firewall installed
  - Have the latest patches
  - Are configured for the highest security

Wireless Penetration Testing

The first step in performing a wireless penetration test is determining which wireless network is the target. This is usually done by conducting wardriving. Depending on the nature of the wireless network and of the target company, there may also be a need for additional steps, such as researching the company on the Web or in the library, or performing social engineering. *Social engineering* is the process of manipulating people into divulging confidential information that they might not give out under normal circumstances. This often involves acting as a user who has lost information.

Wireless Network Attacks

Wardriving

Wardriving is the act of moving around a specific area and mapping the population of wireless access points, as shown in Figure 2-7. Wardriving can be carried out with a laptop with a wireless NIC, antenna (omnidirectional is best), and sniffers, such as Tcpdump, Ethereal, NetStumbler, Airsnort, and WEPCrack. An attacker will usually find APs within a range of 350 feet, but with a more sensitive antenna the attacker can locate APs much farther away. NetStumbler will broadcast probes once each second, waiting for APs to respond.

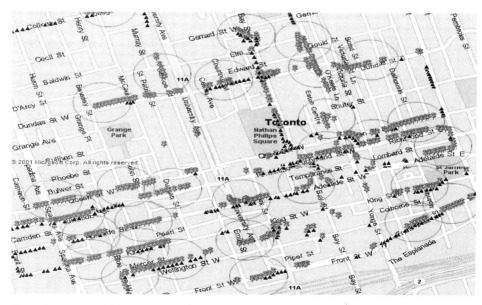

Figure 2-7 Wardriving enables the user to make maps of WLANs in a geographic area.

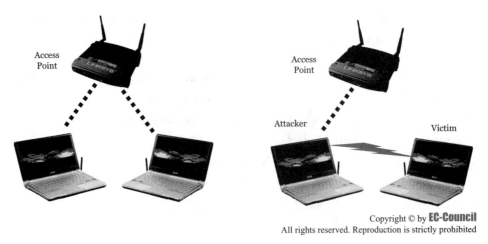

Figure 2-8 Attackers can substitute their own device for an intended AP.

AirSnort and WEPCrack are utilities that can use the captured traffic to compute encryption keys once sufficient packets have been gathered.

WEPCrack is a script that can be run against a file containing raw captured traffic. The key size that is being used by the AP does not matter, because WEPCrack exploits the undersized 24-bit IV value. The user must collect between 100 megabytes and 1 gigabyte of traffic for WEPCrack to crack WEP keystreams, though, so he or she should clear a good amount of available disk space and prepare to collect traffic for a few hours, depending on the amount of traffic that is taking place on the AP.

Man-In-The-Middle Attack

In a man-in-the-middle (MITM) attack, the attacker intercepts identification information of the sending and receiving parties. It substitutes its own key in both situations and allows the attacker to gain access to all information passed between the two parties, as shown in Figure 2-8. Wireless systems are particularly vulnerable to man-in-the-middle attacks. A MITM attack abuses the same weaknesses in the 802.11 specification that have been talked about: the lack of cryptographic acknowledgement for management control and data frames.

Because there is no per-packet authentication in an 802.11 network, frames are easily spoofed with the source of a legitimate client or AP. When the station is disassociated, it will actively scan for new APs. The attacker will offer to authenticate as a legitimate AP on a different channel. The client can offer credentials for authentication, and, no matter what is offered, the AP will accept the client. The client's card may notice that it is on a different channel, but that is often attributed to client roaming. The legitimate AP on a different channel does not know what happened, because there is no MAC conflict.

MITM Attack Design

A typical MITM attack design consists of the following components:

- *The target AP(s)*: To successfully perform a MITM attack, an attacker needs one or more target APs.
- *The wireless-client victims*: The victims of a MITM attack establish an initial wireless connection to the target AP. During the MITM attack, the hacker disconnects the victims from the target AP and has them associate to the MITM AP configured on the attack platform.
- *The MITM attack platform*: The MITM attack platform provides access-point functionality for the wireless clients that were originally connected to the target AP. The MITM attack platform is configured with almost identical settings as the target AP, so a client cannot tell the difference between the attacker's access point and the authorized access point, as shown in Figure 2-9.

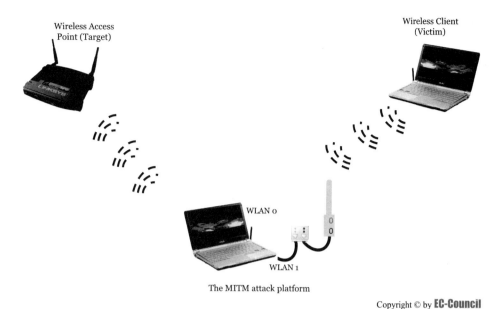

The MITM attack platform

Figure 2-9   The MITM attack platform enables the attacker to simulate the target AP.

MITM Attack Variables

To successfully perform a MITM attack against a wireless network, a few variables come into play. The first variable is how the target AP is configured—specifically, what security features are enabled on the access point to prevent unauthorized access. Before an attack can begin, the following tasks must be accomplished:

- Locate one or more AP(s) with wireless clients already attached.
- Identify the security controls and encryption scheme enabled on the target access point.
- Circumvent the security controls and associate with the target access point.

To establish connectivity and forward client traffic back to the target wireless network, the attacker must be able to circumvent the security controls of the target AP. Without performing this task, it is impossible to forward the client's traffic back to the target access point.

Wireless Network Testing Tools

Detectors

Kismet

Kismet is a free Linux wireless tool. It is an 802.11b wireless network sniffer that is different from a normal network sniffer (such as Ethereal or Tcpdump) because it separates and identifies different wireless networks in an area. Kismet works with any wireless card that is capable of reporting raw packets, including any Prism II–based cards, Cisco Aironet cards, and Orinoco-based cards. Kismet also supports the WSP100 remote sensor by Network Chemistry. Kismet can be used to develop the type of network maps seen in Figure 2-10.

NetStumbler

NetStumbler (Figure 2-11) is the application used most by wardrivers that use a Windows operating system. It has also helped thousands of networking and security specialists design and secure wireless networks.

NetStumbler is a wireless network detector and analysis tool that detects wireless local area networks (WLANs). NetStumbler provides radio frequency (RF) signal information and other data related to computers and radios. It also provides information on the band and data format being used, depending on which wireless networking card is being implemented (802.11b, 802.11a, or 802.11g).

NetStumbler is an active wireless network detection application that does not passively listen for, or receive, beacons. Also, unlike Kismet, NetStumbler does not collect packets.

Figure 2-10 Kismet can be used while wardriving to develop wireless network maps.

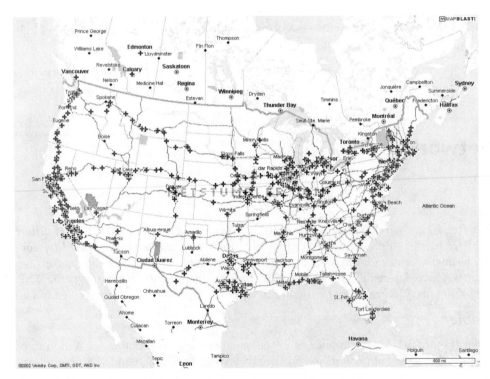

Figure 2-11 NetStumbler is a popular Windows-based wardriving tool.

If NetStumbler detects an infrastructure WLAN, it requests the access point's name. When it finds an ad hoc WLAN, it requests the names of all of the peers it sees.

In addition, the NetStumbler interface provides filtering and analysis tools. These tools allow the user to filter out the number of access points and WLANs based on criteria such as which networks are using encrypted traffic.

Active Versus Passive WLAN Detection   NetStumbler is an active wireless network detection application, which means that it takes a specific action to accomplish WLAN detection. This action sends out a specific data probe called a probe request. The probe request frame and the associated probe response frame are part of the 802.11 standard. Applications that employ passive detection do not broadcast any signals. Instead, these programs listen to the radio band for any 802.11 traffic that is within range of the wireless card. Both approaches have their good points and their bad points.

NetStumbler sends out a probe request and then listens for a probe response from access points or ad hoc networks that are in range. When it answers, the access point responds with information such as the service set identifier (SSID) and the media access control (MAC) address. If the request receives a response, NetStumbler logs the information and reports it to the user via the interface.

Disabling the Beacon   NetStumbler transmits a broadcast request probe to discover a WLAN. Most access points respond to a broadcast request by default. When the access point responds, it transmits its SSID, MAC address, and other information. However, many brands and models of access points allow this feature to be disabled. Once an access point ceases to respond to a request, NetStumbler can no longer detect it.

Running NetStumbler   When NetStumbler starts, it immediately attempts to locate a usable wireless card and a global positioning system (GPS) receiver. The application also opens a new file with extension .ns1. The filename is derived from the date and time when NetStumbler was started and is in YYYYMMDDHHMMSS. ns1 format. If a wireless card is located, the program begins to scan for nearby access points. The data from any located access points are immediately entered into the new file.

Crackers

AirSnort

AirSnort (Figure 2-12) is a Linux-based program that exploits the weak-IV (initialization vector) problem inherent in static WEP. AirSnort implements an algorithm that automates the cracking of static WEP keys by analyzing hundreds of thousands of WEP data packets and identifies approximately 1,500 instances in which the initialization vector section of the packet leaks information about the WEP key in use. Because this attack is based in part on exploiting the limited number of IV pairs used with static WEP, using dynamic WEP or TKIP as the encryption method can prevent it.

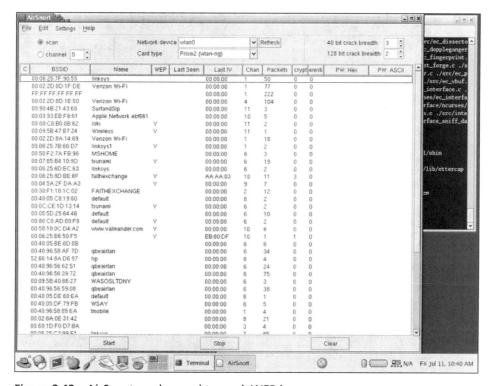

Figure 2-12 AirSnort can be used to crack WEP keys.

WEPCrack

WEPCrack (Figure 2-13) is an open-source tool for breaking 802.11 WEP secret keys. WEPCrack has the following features:

- Database of SSIDs and AP MACs for multiple-IV collection and cracking
- Dynamic WEP determination
- Brute-force capabilities with cracking tool
- Interface with Ethereal that allows Ethereal to use the discovered WEP key to decide WEP traffic for further analysis

Aircrack-ng

The Aircrack-ng tool (Figure 2-14) is a WEP and WPA cracking suite that performs various statistical attacks to discover WEP keys with small amounts of captured data, combined with brute forcing. For cracking WPA/WPA2 preshared keys, a dictionary method is used.

```
------------------------jc-wepcrack 0.9.6 by Johnny Cache-----------------
| Network: 00-30-bd-c0-38-9a        KeySize: 104      Status Running      |
-------------------------------------------------------------------------
| Total Run Time: 0d 0h 0m 10s    Total Compute Time: 0d 0h 3m 30s       |
| Chunksize: 12   Chunks currently out: 7        Current Stragglers: 0    |
| Percent Complete:   ??         Straggler Threshold:  0d 1h 0m 0s        |
-------------------------------------------------------------------------
| Next iKey: 00:00:00:00:00:00:00:00:00:00:d3:e0:00:                      |
-------------------------------------------------------------------------
| Total KeyChunks:        10:00:00:00:00:00:00:00:00:00:00:00:            |
| KeyChunks checked out: 00:00:00:00:00:00:00:00:00:00:0d:51:             |
| KeyChunks checked in:  00:00:00:00:00:00:00:00:00:00:0d:49:             |
-------------------------------------------------------------------------
```

Figure 2-13   WEPCrack is used to crack WEP keys.

```
                       Aircrack-ng 0.5

 1    2    3 4  [00:00:15] Tested 451275 keys (got 566683 IVs)

KB   depth    byte(vote)
 0   0/ 1     AE( 50) 11( 20) 71( 20) 10( 12) 84( 12) 68( 12)
 1   1/ 2     5B( 31) BD( 18) F8( 17) E6( 16) 35( 15) CF( 13)
 2   0/ 3     7F( 31) 74( 24) 54( 17) 1C( 13) 73( 13) 86( 12)
 3   0/ 1     3A(148) EC( 20) EB( 16) FB( 13) F9( 12) 81( 12)
 4   0/ 1     03(140) 90( 31) 4A( 15) 8F( 14) E9( 13) AD( 12)
 5   0/ 1     D0( 69) 04( 27) C8( 24) 60( 24) A1( 20) 26( 20)
 6   0/ 1     AF(124) D4( 29) C8( 20) EE( 18) 54( 12) 3F( 12)
 7   0/ 1     9B(168) 90( 24) 72( 22) F5( 21) 11( 20) F1( 20)
 8   0/ 1     F6(157) EE( 24) 66( 20) EA( 18) DA( 18) E0( 18)
 9   0/ 2     8D( 82) 7B( 44) E2( 30) 11( 27) DE( 23) A4( 20)
10   0/ 1     A5(176) 44( 30) 95( 22) 4E( 21) 94( 21) 4D( 19)

        KEY FOUND! [ AE:5B:7F:3A:03:D0:AF:9B:F6:8D:A5:E2:C7 ]
```

Figure 2-14   The Aircrack-ng tool is a WEP and WPA cracking suite.

Cracking WEP   The following method is used to crack WEP with Aircrack-ng:

1. Start by opening a console window.
2. On the command line, launch Aircrack-ng using the following syntax:

```
aircrack-ng -a 1 <filename.cap>
```

The user can specify multiple input files (either in .cap or .ivs format). The Aircrack-ng tool's available options can be seen in Figure 2-15.

Man-In-The-Middle Attack Tool
Monkey-Jack

Monkey-Jack is a tool that manipulates layer 1 and 2 and allows for a MITM insertion-based attack on a victim device. The victim device believes that it is communicating with the access point when in fact all communication is being effectively proxied through the attacker's connection.

Other Tools
NetworkView

NetworkView (Figure 2-16) is a small program that is designed to locate network devices and routes using Transmission Control Protocol/Internet Protocol (TCP/IP), Domain Name Service (DNS), Simple Network Management Protocol (SNMP), port scanning, NetBIOS, and Windows Management Interface (WMI). Once the user has gained access to the actual wireless network, it helps to know the network topology, including the names of other computers and the devices on the network.

NetworkView can be used to accomplish the following tasks:

- Discover TCP/IP nodes and routes
- Get MAC addresses and NIC manufacturer names
- Monitor nodes and receive alerts
- Produce printed maps and reports
- Control and secure networks with the SNMP MIB browser, the WMI browser, and the port scanner

Option	Param.	Description
-a	amode	Force attack mode (1 = static WEP, 2 = WPA/WPA2-PSK).
-e	essid	If set, all IVs from networks with the same ESSID will be used. This option is also required for WPA/WPA2-PSK cracking if the ESSID is not broadcasted (hidden).
-b	bssid	Select the target network based on the access point's MAC address.
-p	nbcpu	On SMP systems: # of CPU to use.
-q	none	Enable quiet mode (no status output until the key is found, or not).
-c	none	(WEP cracking) Restrict the search space to alpha-numeric characters only (0×20 - 0x7F).
-t	none	(WEP cracking) Restrict the search space to binary coded decimal hex characters.
-h	none	(WEP cracking) Restrict the search space to numeric characters (0×30-0×39) These keys are used by default in most Fritz!BOXes.
-d	start	(WEP cracking) Set the beginning of the WEP key (in hex), for debugging purposes.
-m	maddr	(WEP cracking) MAC address to filter WEP data packets. Alternatively, specify -m ff:ff:ff:ff:ff:ff to use all and every IVs, regardless of the network.
-n	nbits	(WEP cracking) Specify the length of the key: 64 for 40-bit WEP, 128 for 104-bit WEP, etc. The default value is 128.
-i	index	(WEP cracking) Only keep the IVs that have this key index (1 to 4). The default behaviour is to ignore the key index.
-f	fudge	(WEP cracking) By default, this parameter is set to 2 for 104-bit WEP and to 5 for 40-bit WEP. Specify a higher value to increase the bruteforce level: cracking will take more time, but with a higher likelihood of success.
-k	korek	(WEP cracking) There are 17 korek statistical attacks. Sometimes one attack creates a huge false positive that prevents the key from being found, even with lots of IVs. Try -k 1, -k 2, ... -k 17 to disable each attack selectively.
-x/-x0	none	(WEP cracking) Disable last keybytes brutforce.
-x1	none	(WEP cracking) Enable last keybyte bruteforcing (default).
-x2	none	(WEP cracking) Enable last two keybytes bruteforcing.
-X	none	(WEP cracking) Disable bruteforce multithreading (SMP only).
-y	none	(WEP cracking) This is an experimental single bruteforce attack which should only be used when the standard attack mode fails with more than one million IVs
-w	words	(WPA cracking) Path to a wordlist or "-" without the quotes for standard in (stdin).

Figure 2-15   The Aircrack-ng tool includes a number of options for cracking WEP and WPA keys.

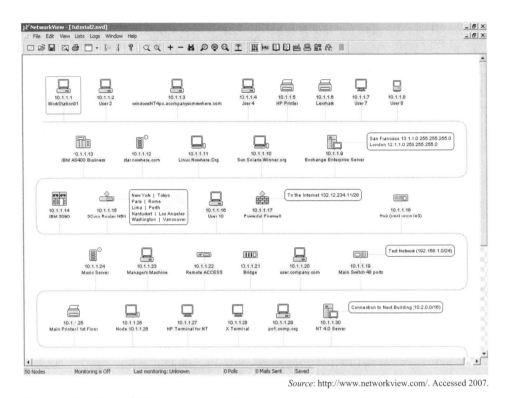

Source: http://www.networkview.com/. Accessed 2007.

Figure 2-16 NetworkView can be used to locate network devices and routes.

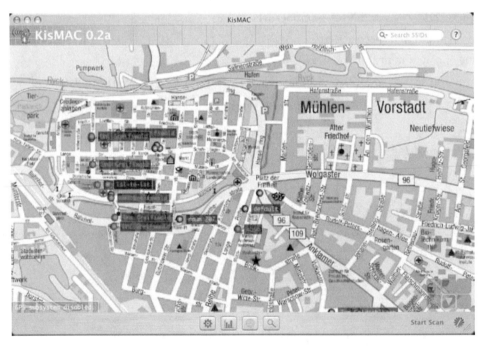

Figure 2-17 KisMAC can be used for wardriving on the Mac.

KisMAC

KisMAC (Figure 2-17) is a wardriving and WLAN discovery and penetration testing tool available on the Macintosh platform. Most wardriving applications provide the capability to discover networks in either active mode or passive mode; KisMAC provides both.

In addition to being used as a wardriving application, KisMAC can also be used for wireless network penetration testing. KisMAC has built-in functionality to perform many of the most common WLAN attacks. Additionally, KisMAC can import packet capture dumps from other programs to perform many offline attacks against wireless networks.

Attacking WEP Encryption with KisMAC   KisMAC has three primary methods of WEP cracking built in:

1. Word-list attacks

2. Weak-scheduling attacks

3. Brute-force attacks

To use one of these attacks, the user has to generate enough initialization vectors (IVs) for the attack to work. The easiest way to do this is by reinjecting traffic, which is usually accomplished by capturing an Address Resolution Protocol (ARP) packet, spoofing the sender, and sending it back to the access point. This generates a large amount of traffic that can then be captured and decoded. Unfortunately, the user cannot always capture an ARP packet under normal circumstances; however, when a client authenticates to the access point, an ARP packet is usually generated. Because of this, if the user can deauthenticate the clients who are on the network and cause them to reassociate, the user may get the ARP packet.

Two hosts are required to successfully crack the WEP key:

1. One host is used to inject traffic.

2. The other host is used to capture the traffic (specifically the IVs).

In this case, the user will use KisMAC to inject and will have a second host to capture the traffic.

Attacking WPA with KisMAC   Unlike WEP, which requires a large amount of traffic to be generated in order to crack the key, cracking WPA only requires that the user capture the four-way Extensible Authentication Protocol Over Local Area Network (EAPOL) handshake at authentication.

Also, unlike cracking WEP, the WPA attack is an offline dictionary attack, which means that when the user uses KisMAC to crack a WPA preshared key, the user only needs to capture a small amount of traffic; the actual attack can be carried out later, even when the user is out of range of the access point, as shown in Figure 2-18.

WPA is only vulnerable when a short passphrase is used. Even then, it must be a dictionary word or one that is in the KisMAC user's word list. An extensive word list with many combinations of letters, numbers, and special characters can help increase the odds of successfully cracking WPA.

To attempt a dictionary attack against KisMAC, the user may need to deauthenticate clients. However, when attempting dictionary attacks against WPA, everything can be done from one host, which will cause the client to disassociate from the network and force it to reconnect. This requires the four-way EAPOL handshake to be transmitted again.

Dnsmasq

Dnsmasq is a lightweight, easily configured Domain Name System (DNS) forwarder and Dynamic Host Configuration Protocol (DHCP) server. Dnsmasq serves two important functions on the user's attack platform:

1. Provides IP addresses to the wireless clients connecting to the user's access point

2. Gives the ability to monitor and poison DNS queries

Figure 2-18   KisMAC can perform attacks on WPA even when offline.

This tool is very useful when redirecting DNS requests for Web applications to the user's spoofed Web server. Dnsmasq can be used on Linux and Mac platforms.

Airpwn

Airpwn is a supporting tool for 802.11 (wireless) packet injection. Using a traditional 802.11 network, the user can send data to the AP (access point) and also receive replies from the AP. Airpwn captures incoming wireless packets and injects content into those packets, thus spoofing replies from the AP and tricking the client into believing that Airpwn is the AP.

Hardware Tools

To successfully perform a MITM attack, the user needs several pieces of hardware and a few key software programs, as shown in Figure 2-19. A typical MITM attack platform utilizes the following hardware components:

- A laptop computer with two PCMCIA (Personal Computer Memory Cards International Association) slots, or one PCMCIA and one mini-PCI (Peripheral Component Interconnect) slot
- Two wireless network interface cards (NICs)
- An external antenna (omnidirectional preferred)
- A bi-directional amplifier (optional)
- Pigtails to connect the external antennae to the amplifier and wireless NIC
- A handheld global positioning system (GPS) unit (optional)
- A power inverter

Laptop

The laptop serves as a clone of the target AP and provides connectivity back to the target wireless network. The platform also runs a Web server to host any spoofed Web sites during an attack. Therefore, the laptop should be well equipped to handle memory-intensive tasks.

Figure 2-19   Man-in-the-middle attacks require specific hardware as well as software.

Wireless Network Cards

Two wireless network cards are required for an attack platform. One wireless card provides access point functionality for wireless clients (victims), and must be able to go into Host AP mode (also known as master mode). The second wireless card provides connectivity to the target AP.

Antennas

Wireless connectivity to the target AP and the wireless clients is essential for a man-in-the-middle attack to work. Also, the user needs to have a strong wireless signal broadcasting from the second wireless card. Therefore, choosing the right antenna is important. There are two main types of antennas to consider for this attack: directional and omnidirectional antennas.

Amplifying the Wireless Signal

A 2.4-GHz amplifier is designed to extend the range of a 2.4-GHz radio device or an AP. The amplifier is used in conjunction with an antenna to boost the signal of the user's MITM access point. The intent is for the wireless signal access point to be stronger than the wireless signal of the target access point. A typical amplifier has two connectors; one connection is made to the wireless card, and the other connects to the antenna.

Figures 2-20 and 2-21 demonstrate the wireless signal of a target access point compared to the wireless signal of the MITM access point using a 9-dBi omnidirectional antenna and a 1-watt amplifier.

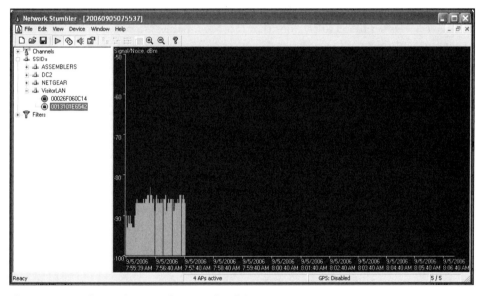

Figure 2-20   This is the signal strength of the target access point.

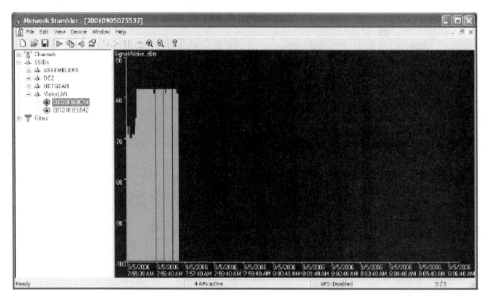

Figure 2-21　This is the signal strength of the user's access point.

Chapter Summary

- Wireless, by its very nature, has no well-defined perimeter, making security more challenging.

- Vendors have SSIDs set to default values that most companies do not change, so attackers can easily guess them, even if they are not broadcast.

- The 802.11 standards are a set of standards for WLAN. They denote an over-the-air interface between a wireless client and a base station or access point.

- Spread spectrum communications are data signals that are spread across a wider frequency bandwidth of the radio channel.

- A typical wireless infrastructure comprises devices that connect to the network. These devices include antennas, access points, mobile stations, base station subsystems, network subsystems, a base station controller, a terminal, a mobile switching center, a wireless modem, and a wireless router.

- The RADIUS shared secret is vulnerable to an offline dictionary attack, based on the capture of the response authenticator or message-authenticator attribute. Changing the shared secret between authentication methods will fix this vulnerability. It also can be vulnerable to a brute-force attack.

- All the users in wireless broadband channels use the same frequency but have a different chipping sequence.

- The IV is a value that is used to randomize the keystream value, and each packet has an IV value. The standard only allows 24 bits, which can be used up within hours at a busy AP. Thus, IV values will be reused and vulnerable to attack.

- Wardriving can be carried out with a laptop with a wireless NIC, antenna (omnidirectional is best), and sniffers.

Review Questions

1. How are wireless networks more vulnerable than wired networks?

_____

_____

_____

_____

2. How are the 802.11 standard variations (a, b, g, and n) different from each other?

_____

_____

_____

_____

3. What are the two methods of spread-spectrum broadcasting?

_____

_____

_____

_____

4. What are the hardware components of a wireless network?

_____

_____

_____

_____

5. Describe the vulnerabilities of RADIUS.

_____

_____

_____

_____

6. How can WEP encryption be cracked?

_____

_____

_____

_____

7. What are the vulnerabilities of WPA2?

_____

_____

_____

_____

8. What is the goal of wardriving?

_____

_____

_____

_____

9. Describe the steps in a man-in-the-middle attack.

_____

_____

_____

_____

10. Describe the hardware requirements for conducting a man-in-the-middle attack.

_____

_____

_____

_____

Hands-On Projects

1. Perform the following steps:

   ▪ Navigate to Chapter 2 of the Student Resource Center. Copy the file aircrack-ng-0.9.3-win.zip to your system or download the latest stable version from *http://www.aircrackng.org*.

   ▪ Unzip the contents of the Aircrack-ng zip file to the hard drive. This will create a directory called aircrack-ng-0.9.3-win.

   ▪ To use the Aircrack-ng suite, open Windows Explorer and double-click Aircrack-ng GUI.exe in the bin subdirectory of aircrack-ng-0.9.3-win. See Figures 2-22 and 2-23.

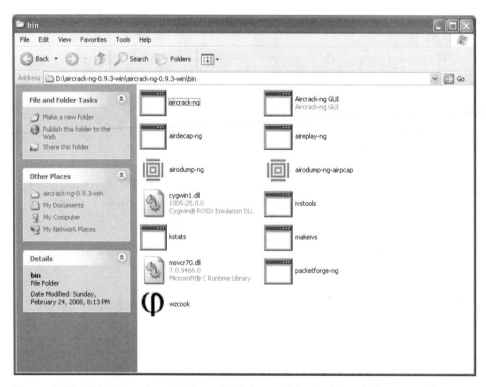

Figure 2-22 The Aircrack-ng GUI.exe file is located in the bin subdirectory of aircrack-ng-0.9.3-win.

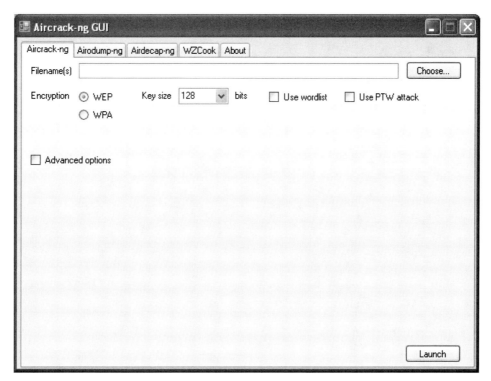

Figure 2-23   Explore the Aircrack-ng suite.

## Chapter 3

VoIP Penetration Testing

Objectives

After completing this chapter, you should be able to:

- Assess VoIP vulnerabilities
- Perform VoIP penetration testing
- Use tools to perform VoIP penetration testing

Key Terms

Stack fingerprinting   the process of observing the way systems respond to network requests in order to determine the targets' operating systems and firmware versions

Introduction to VoIP Penetration Testing

In many homes and organizations, traditional phone lines have been replaced by voice over IP (VoIP) systems, which use the Internet to send voice calls between parties. Much like any other form of networking, VoIP has vulnerabilities. This chapter teaches you how to test a VoIP system for many of these known vulnerabilities.

Vulnerability Assessment

When performing the initial vulnerability assessment for a VoIP system, it is not necessary to test every single IP phone for every vulnerability. Testing one phone per vendor is usually enough, because configurations should be functionally identical. In most VoIP environments, it is possible to identify IP phones by their SNMP signature. Calling the IP phone directly, bypassing any gateways or gatekeepers, can sometimes yield interesting information, such as caller ID, physical location, SNMP community, and IP address.

VoIP Risks and Vulnerabilities

VoIP security threats can be divided into the following three categories:

1. *Attacks against the VoIP devices*: Devices used for VoIP are still subject to all of their operating systems' vulnerabilities.

2. *Configuration faults in VoIP devices*: The default settings of many VoIP devices are insecure and may expose TCP and UDP ports to attacks.

3. *IP infrastructure attacks*: The availability of VoIP services is dependent upon the IP infrastructure. Any attack to this infrastructure, such as a DDoS, may harm the VoIP services and impact all VoIP communication. Packets are transported using TCP and UDP in VoIP, so if these protocols are attacked, it may affect the VoIP services.

The following are various VoIP attacks:

- *Reconnaissance attacks*: There are two types of reconnaissance attacks: call walking and port scanning. In call walking, attackers initiate sequential calls to a block of telephone numbers in order to identify vulnerabilities. Port-scanning attacks scan sequential ports for the same purpose.

- *Protocol fuzzing*: In protocol fuzzing, an attacker sends a message that looks genuine, but in reality, the message is broken or fuzzed. If the target system parses this message, it may cause a variety of failures.

- *Denial-of-service (DoS) attacks*: A denial-of-service (DoS) attack occurs when an attacker sends a large amount of traffic to a target system in order to overload its capacity. This exhausts the system's resources and denies service to its users.

- *Call hijacking and redirection*: Man-in-the-middle attacks and node spoofing make it easier for an attacker to hijack and redirect calls. These techniques allow the attacker to receive, eavesdrop on, and redirect calls before they reach the intended recipient.

- *VoIP spam*: VoIP spam, or spam over Internet telephony (SPIT), occurs when an attacker sends unwanted bulk messages to users on a VoIP network. These attacks are very difficult to track and include unauthorized resource use and privacy violations. They can be from outsiders such as spammers or hackers or even from insiders such as infected PCs or e-mail attachments.

- *Spoofing*: Spoofing involves making calls while pretending to be someone else. This can be done by deliberately inserting falsified data into the packet headers and hiding the original data.

- *Eavesdropping*: Eavesdropping is the unauthorized monitoring of voice packets. Network protocol analyzers, sniffers, and packet capture tools are readily available and useful for eavesdropping.

- *Session anomalies*: In this attack, the attacker disturbs the flow of the message packets in order to make it impossible for the user or server to handle the call.

VoIP Penetration Testing Steps

Step 1: Eavesdropping

There are various tools available for capturing, rebuilding, and replaying VoIP conversations, which can be useful for VoIP administrators and penetration testers. These tools decode signaling messages in Real-time Transport Protocol (RTP) media streams or voice packets. Some of these tools include:

- vomit
- VoIPong (along with sniffers such as Ethereal)
- pcapsipdump

Step 2: Flooding and Logic Attacks

A TCP synchronization flood exploits the TCP connection process. Spoofed IP addresses do not return acknowledgment packets, so their requests remain in the queue. Sending many of these requests will overload the system. Penetration testers can use flooding techniques like Session Initiation Protocol (SIP) INVITE or REGISTER packets to overload devices with VoIP protocol packets. Tools such as InviteFlood and IAXFlood can also be used.

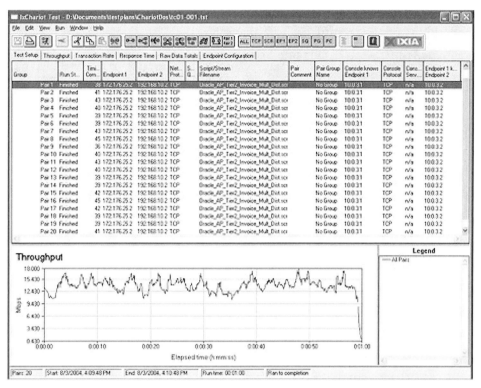

Figure 3-1   IxChariot can be used to launch a DoS attack.

Step 3: Denial-Of-Service (DoS) Attack

This attack allows users to deliberately send a large number of useless messages from either a single location or from multiple locations to the target, overloading the target and denying service to legitimate users. The risk of DoS attacks can be reduced by using strong firewalls. To initiate a DoS attack to test a VoIP system, testers can use the IxChariot tool (Figure 3-1).

Step 4: Call Hijacking and Redirection Attacks

In these types of attacks, attackers manipulate the registration of the victim's SIP URL to take control of all the victim's calls. To test for these attacks, penetration testers can encrypt SIP over Transport Layer Security (TLS) or use IPSec on the VoIP network. They then check for 3*xx* response code classes to redirect the victim's calls and inform him or her of further actions, such as redirecting the calls to a new number (the attacker's phone).

Step 5: ICMP Ping Sweeps

ICMP ping sweeps are an easy way to find active hosts. Pinging includes sending ICMP type 8 packets (ICMP ECHO REQUEST) to an IP address. If ICMP is not blocked by the router or firewall, the host will reply with an ICMP type 0 packet (ICMP ECHO REPLY).

There are many tools for running ICMP ping sweeps, including the following:

- fping
- Nmap
- SuperScan
- Nessus

In the following example, fping is used with the command-line option -g to specify the range of hosts to scan, along with the -a option to return results from live hosts:

```
fping -a -g 192.168.1.0/24
192.168.1.21
192.168.1.22
192.168.1.24
192.168.1.25
192.168.1.23
192.168.1.27
192.168.1.51
192.168.1.52
192.168.1.53
192.168.1.54
192.168.1.56
192.168.1.57
192.168.1.103
192.168.1.104
```

The following example uses another tool, Nmap, along with the -sP option to designate a ping sweep:

```
nmap -sP 192.168.1.1-254
Starting Nmap 4.01 (http://www.insecure.org/nmap/) at 2006-02-19
20:51 CST
Host 192.168.1.1 appears to be up.
MAC Address: 00:13:10:D4:AF:44 (Cisco-Linksys)
Host 192.168.1.21 appears to be up.
MAC Address: 00:04:13:24:23:8D (Snom Technology AG)
Host 192.168.1.22 appears to be up.
MAC Address: 00:0F:34:11:80:45 (Cisco Systems)
Host 192.168.1.23 appears to be up.
MAC Address: 00:15:62:86:BA:3E (Cisco Systems)
Host 192.168.1.24 appears to be up.
MAC Address: 00:0E:08:DA:DA:17 (Sipura Technology)
Host 192.168.1.25 appears to be up.
MAC Address: 00:0B:82:06:4D:37 (Grandstream Networks)
Host 192.168.1.27 appears to be up.
MAC Address: 00:04:F2:03:15:46 (Polycom)
Host 192.168.1.51 appears to be up.
MAC Address: 00:04:13:23:34:95 (Snom Technology AG)
Host 192.168.1.52 appears to be up.
```

```
MAC Address: 00:15:62:EA:69:E8 (Cisco Systems)

Host 192.168.1.53 appears to be up.

MAC Address: 00:04:0D:50:40:B0 (Avaya)

Host 192.168.1.54 appears to be up.

MAC Address: 00:0E:08:DA:24:AE (Sipura Technology)

Host 192.168.1.55 appears to be up.

MAC Address: 00:E0:11:03:03:97 (Uniden SAN Diego R&D Center)

Host 192.168.1.56 appears to be up.

MAC Address: 00:0D:61:0B:EA:36 (Giga-Byte Technology Co.)

Host 192.168.1.57 appears to be up.

MAC Address: 00:01:E1:02:C8:DB (Kinpo Electronics)

Host 192.168.1.103 appears to be up.

MAC Address: 00:09:7A:44:15:DB (Louis Design Labs.)

Host 192.168.1.104 appears to be up.

Nmap finished: 254 IP addresses (17 hosts up) scanned in 5.329 seconds
```

Step 6: ARP Pings

When scanning a local Ethernet subnet, it is simple to compile a map of MAC addresses to IP addresses, which enables an attacker to perform man-in-the-middle and hijacking attacks. On the local LAN, testers can use an ARP broadcast frame to request MAC addresses corresponding to a large range of IP addresses in order to determine whether the hosts are alive on the local network. There are many tools that can perform ARP pings, including Nmap and the MAC Address Discovery tool from SolarWinds.

Arping is a command-line tool for ARP pinging IP addresses and MAC addresses; the following example shows a sample command-line string and its corresponding output:

```
arping -I eth0 -c 2 192.168.100.17

ARPING 192.168.100.17 from 192.168.100.254 eth0

Unicast reply from 192.168.100.17 [00:80:C8:E8:4B:8E]  8.419ms

Unicast reply from 192.168.100.17 [00:80:C8:E8:4B:8E]  2.095ms

Sent 2 probes (1 broadcast(s))

Received 2 response(s)
```

Step 7: TCP Ping Scans

A TCP ping scan involves sending a TCP SYN-flagged or ACK-flagged packet to a commonly used TCP port on the target host. If an RST packet is returned, the host is alive at the target IP address. ACK packets are more useful, because they can be used to bypass stateless firewalls that monitor only for incoming SYNs. By default, Nmap uses a SYN packet on port 80 to probe, but it can be customized from the command line to use an ACK packet on a different port using the -PT option, as shown in the following example:

```
nmap -P0 -PT80 192.168.1.23

Starting Nmap 4.01 (http://www.insecure.org/nmap/) at 2006-02-19 21:28 CST

Interesting ports on 192.168.1.23:

(The 1671 ports scanned but not shown below are in state: closed)

PORT STATE SERVICE
```

```
80/tcp open http

MAC Address: 00:15:62:86:BA:3E (Cisco Systems)

Nmap finished: one IP address (1 host up) scanned in 2.144 seconds
```

Another tool used for TCP pinging is Hping2. The following example shows Hping2 being used to scan on port 80:

```
hping 192.168.1.104 -A -p 80

HPING 192.168.1.103 (eth0 192.168.1.103): A set, 40 headers + 0 data bytes

len=40 ip=192.168.1.103 ttl=64 DF id=0 sport=80 flags=R seq=0 win=0
rtt=0.1 ms

len=40 ip=192.168.1.103 ttl=64 DF id=1 sport=80 flags=R seq=1 win=0
rtt=0.1 ms

len=40 ip=192.168.1.103 ttl=64 DF id=2 sport=80 flags=R seq=2 win=0
rtt=0.0 ms

len=40 ip=192.168.1.103 ttl=64 DF id=3 sport=80 flags=R seq=3 win=0
rtt=0.1 ms

len=40 ip=192.168.1.103 ttl=64 DF id=4 sport=80 flags=R seq=4 win=0
rtt=0.0 ms

len=40 ip=192.168.1.103 ttl=64 DF id=5 sport=80 flags=R seq=5 win=0
rtt=0.0 ms

len=40 ip=192.168.1.103 ttl=64 DF id=6 sport=80 flags=R seq=6 win=0
rtt=0.0 ms
```

In the output above, *flags=R* shows TCP RST packets received from the target on port 80, which indicates a live host.

Step 8: SNMP Sweeps

Simple Network Management Protocol (SNMP) scanning is another effective method of determining active network equipment. SNMP is an application-layer protocol that can monitor and control network devices. SNMP v1 and v2 are based on a very simple form of authentication called community strings (essentially, plaintext passwords), while SNMP v3 is based on stronger encryption such as AES and 3DES.

Many administrators neglect to modify the default community strings on their network devices, allowing attackers to easily break in to them. Usually, SNMP scans return a great amount of information by simply trying these default passwords.

SNMP scanning tools include SNMP Sweep, SNScan, and command-line tools for UNIX-based systems such as snmpwalk, Nomad, Cheops, and snmpenum.

Step 9: Port Scanning and Service Discovery

After an attacker discovers active IP addresses using host discovery techniques, he or she can investigate each address for its corresponding listening services. VoIP primarily uses TCP and UDP ports, so attackers may scan these ports in order to search for active services. Attackers can then try to interact with these services to gain information about the VoIP network. Common TCP services include the following:

- WWW (port 80)
- FTP (ports 20 and 21)
- SMTP (port 25)

Common UDP services include the following:

- DNS (port 53)
- SNMP (ports 161 and 162)
- DHCP (ports 7 and 68)

TCP SYN Scan

Nmap is a port scanner that supports several different types of scans, including TCP SYN scanning and UDP scanning, in one utility. In a TCP SYN scan, the attacker sends a TCP SYN packet to a specific port, attempting to establish a TCP connection with the target host. A returned SYN/ACK-flagged TCP packet indicates the port is open, while an RST packet indicates a closed port.

The following example shows a simple TCP SYN scan with Nmap:

```
nmap 192.168.1.103

Starting Nmap 4.01 (http://www.insecure.org/nmap/) at 2006-02-24 09:12 CST

Interesting ports on [192.168.1.103]:

(The 1662 ports scanned but not shown below are in state: filtered)

PORT STATE SERVICE

22/tcp closed ssh

23/tcp closed telnet

80/tcp open http

443/tcp open https

1720/tcp open H.323/Q.931

2000/tcp open callbook

2001/tcp open dc

2002/tcp open globe
```

The -sV option can be used with Nmap for service detection, as shown in the following example:

```
nmap -sV 192.168.1.103

Starting Nmap 4.01 (http://www.insecure.org/nmap/) at 2006-02-30 15:13 CST

Interesting ports on 192.168.1.103:

(The 1662 ports scanned but not shown below are in state: filtered)

PORT STATE SERVICE VERSION

22/tcp closed ssh

23/tcp closed telnet

80/tcp open http Microsoft IIS webserver 5.0

443/tcp open ssl/http Microsoft IIS webserver 5.0

1720/tcp open tcpwrapped

2000/tcp open callbook?

2001/tcp open dc?

2002/tcp open globe?

Service Info: OS: Windows

Nmap finished: one IP address (1 host up) scanned in 112.869 seconds.
```

Using Nmap with the default options facilitates making critical VoIP services fully functional with little or no record of the scan, as in the following example:

```
nmap -P0 -sV 192.168.1.103
```

```
Starting Nmap 4.01 (http://www.insecure.org/nmap/) at 2006-02-19 21:49 CST

Interesting ports on 192.168.1.103:

(The 1666 ports scanned but not shown below are in state: closed)

PORT STATE SERVICE VERSION

21/tcp open ftp vsftpd 1.2.1

22/tcp open ssh OpenSSH 3.6.1p2 (protocol 1.99)

80/tcp open http Apache httpd 2.0.46 ((CentOS))

111/tcp open rpcbind 2 (rpc #100000)

113/tcp open ident authd

3306/tcp open mysql MySQL (unauthorized)

MAC Address: 00:09:7A:44:15:DB (Louis Design Labs.)

Service Info: OS: Unix

Nmap finished: one IP address (1 host up) scanned in 6.437 seconds.
```

UDP Scan

In a UDP scan, an attacker sends an empty UDP header to each UDP port on the target. If a port responds with a UDP packet, an active service is listening. An ICMP port unreachable error indicates that the port is unused or filtered. In Nmap, a UDP scan can identify the other ports running on the network, as shown in the following example:

nmap -sU 192.168.1.103

```
Starting Nmap 4.01 (http://www.insecure.org/nmap/) at 2006-02-20 05:26 EST

(The 1473 ports scanned but not shown below are in state: closed)

PORT STATE SERVICE

67/udp open|filtered dhcpserver

69/udp open|filtered tftp

111/udp open|filtered rpcbind

123/udp open|filtered ntp

784/udp open|filtered unknown

5060/udp open|filtered sip

32768/udp open|filtered omad

Nmap finished: one IP address (1 host up) scanned in 1.491 seconds.
```

The above results show that this server supports both DCHP and TFTP services (UDP ports 67 and 69, respectively).

Step 10: Host/Device Identification

Once the open TCP and UDP ports have been identified on a range of targets, the next step is to determine the operating systems and firmware versions of the targets. *Stack fingerprinting* is an effective method for doing this, in which the attacker observes the way the systems respond to network requests. Different operating systems and firmware versions respond to requests in different ways. Nmap has a built-in OS detection option, -O, shown in the following example:

nmap -O -P0 192.168.1.1-254

```
Starting Nmap 4.01 at 2006-02-20 01:03 CST
```

Interesting ports on 192.168.1.21:

(The 1670 ports scanned but not shown below are in state: closed)

Port State Service

80/tcp open http

443/tcp open https

MAC Address: 00:04:13:24:23:8D (Snom Technology AG)

Device type: general purpose

Running: Linux 2.4.X|2.5.X

OS details: Linux 2.4.0 - 2.5.20

Uptime 0.264 days (since Sun Feb 19 18:43:56 2006)

Interesting ports on 192.168.1.22:

(The 1671 ports scanned but not shown below are in state: filtered)

Port State Service

23/tcp open telnet

MAC Address: 00:0F:34:11:80:45 (Cisco Systems)

Device type: VoIP phone

Running: Cisco embedded

OS details: Cisco IP phone (POS3-04-3-00, PC030301)

Interesting ports on 192.168.1.23:

(The 1671 ports scanned but not shown below are in state: closed)

Port State Service

80/tcp open http

MAC Address: 00:15:62:86:BA:3E (Cisco Systems)

Device type: VoIP phone|VoIP adapter

Running: Cisco embedded

OS details: Cisco VoIP Phone 7905/7912 or ATA 186 Analog Telephone Adapter

Interesting ports on 192.168.1.24:

(The 1671 ports scanned but not shown below are in state: closed)

Port State Service

80/tcp open http

MAC Address: 00:0E:08:DA:DA:17 (Sipura Technology)

Device type: VoIP adapter

Running: Sipura embedded

OS details: Sipura SPA-841/1000/2000/3000 POTS<->VoIP gateway

Interesting ports on 192.168.1.25:

(The 1670 ports scanned but not shown below are in state: filtered)

Port State Service

```
80/tcp open http

4144/tcp closed wincim

MAC Address: 00:0B:82:06:4D:37 (Grandstream Networks)

TCP/IP fingerprint:

SInfo(V=4.01%P=i686-pc-linux-gnu%D=2/20%Tm=43F96A02%O=80%C=4144%M=000B82)

TSeq(Class=TD%gcd=1%SI=1%IPID=I%TS=U)

T1(Resp=Y%DF=Y%W=109%ACK=S++%Flags=AS%Ops=M)

T2(Resp=Y%DF=Y%W=C00%ACK=S++%Flags=AR%Ops=)

T2(Resp=Y%DF=Y%W=800%ACK=S++%Flags=AR%Ops=)

T2(Resp=Y%DF=Y%W=C00%ACK=S++%Flags=AR%Ops=)

T3(Resp=Y%DF=Y%W=109%ACK=S++%Flags=AS%Ops=M)

T4(Resp=Y%DF=Y%W=400%ACK=S++%Flags=AR%Ops=)

T5(Resp=Y%DF=Y%W=C00%ACK=S++%Flags=AR%Ops=)

T5(Resp=Y%DF=Y%W=1000%ACK=S++%Flags=AR%Ops=)

T5(Resp=Y%DF=Y%W=800%ACK=S++%Flags=AR%Ops=)

T6(Resp=Y%DF=Y%W=C00%ACK=S++%Flags=AR%Ops=)

T6(Resp=Y%DF=Y%W=400%ACK=S++%Flags=AR%Ops=)

T7(Resp=Y%DF=Y%W=800%ACK=S++%Flags=AR%Ops=)

T7(Resp=Y%DF=Y%W=400%ACK=S++%Flags=AR%Ops=)

T7(Resp=Y%DF=Y%W=C00%ACK=S++%Flags=AR%Ops=)

PU(Resp=Y%DF=N%TOS=0%IPLEN=38%RIPTL=148%RID=E%RIPCK=E%UCK=E%ULEN=134%
DAT=E)

Interesting ports on 192.168.1.27:

(The 1670 ports scanned but not shown below are in state: closed)

Port State Service

80/tcp open http

5060/tcp open sip

MAC Address: 00:04:F2:03:15:46 (Polycom)

Device type: X terminal|load balancer

Running: Neoware NetOS, HP embedded, Cisco embedded

OS details: Cisco 11151/Arrowpoint 150 load balancer, Neoware (was HDS)

NetOS V. 2.0.1 or HP Entria C3230A

Interesting ports on 192.168.1.51:

(The 1670 ports scanned but not shown below are in state: closed)

Port State Service

80/tcp open http

443/tcp open https

MAC Address: 00:04:13:23:34:95 (Snom Technology AG)

Device type: general purpose
```

```
Running: Linux 2.4.X|2.5.X

OS details: Linux 2.4.0 - 2.5.20

Uptime 0.265 days (since Sun Feb 19 18:43:55 2006)

Interesting ports on 192.168.1.52:

(The 1671 ports scanned but not shown below are in state: filtered)

Port State Service

23/tcp open telnet

MAC Address: 00:15:62:EA:69:E8 (Cisco Systems)

Device type: VoIP phone

Running: Cisco embedded

OS details: Cisco IP phone (POS3-04-3-00, PC030301)

All 1672 scanned ports on 192.168.1.53 are: closed.

MAC Address: 00:04:0D:50:40:B0

Many fingerprints match this host that provides specific OS details.

Interesting ports on 192.168.1.54:

(The 1671 ports scanned but not shown below are in state: closed).

Port State Service

80/tcp open http

MAC Address: 00:0E:08:DA:24:AE (Sipura Technology)

Device type: VoIP adapter

Running: Sipura embedded

OS details: Sipura SPA-841/1000/2000/3000 POTS<->VoIP gateway

All 1672 scanned ports on 192.168.1.55 are: closed

MAC Address: 00:E0:11:03:03:97 (Uniden SAN Diego R&D Center)

Aggressive OS guesses: NetJet Version 3.0 - 4.0 Printer (94%), Cray

UNICOS/mk 8.6 (93%), Intel NetportExpress XL Print Server (93%), Kyocera

IB-21 Printer NIC (93%), Kyocera Printer (network module IB-21E 1.3.x)

(93%), OkiData 20nx printer with OkiLAN ethernet module (93%), Okidata 7200

Printer (93%), Okidata OKI C5100 Laser Printer (93%), Okidata OKI C7200

Printer (93%), Zebra Technologies TLP2844-Z printer (93%)

No exact OS matches for host (test conditions non-ideal).

Interesting ports on 192.168.1.56:

(The 1669 ports scanned but not shown below are in state: closed).

Port State Service

135/tcp open msrpc

139/tcp open netbios-ssn

1005/tcp open unknown

MAC Address: 00:0D:61:0B:EA:36 (Giga-Byte Technology Co.)
```

Device type: general purpose

Running: Microsoft Windows 2003/.NET|NT/2K/XP

OS details: Microsoft Windows 2003 Server or XP SP2

Interesting ports on 192.168.1.57:

(The 1670 ports scanned but not shown below are in state: closed.)

Port State Service

80/tcp open http

5060/tcp open sip

MAC Address: 00:01:E1:02:C8:DB (Kinpo Electronics)

TCP/IP fingerprint:

SInfo(V=4.01%P=i686-pc-linux-gnu%D=2/20%Tm=43F96A29%O=80%C=1%M=0001E1)

TSeq(Class=TD%gcd=9C4%SI=0%IPID=I%TS=U)

TSeq(Class=TD%gcd=9C4%SI=1%IPID=I%TS=U)

TSeq(Class=TD%gcd=9C4%SI=0%IPID=I%TS=U)

T1(Resp=Y%DF=N%W=578%ACK=S++%Flags=AS%Ops=M)

T2(Resp=N)

T3(Resp=Y%DF=N%W=578%ACK=S++%Flags=AS%Ops=M)

T4(Resp=Y%DF=N%W=0%ACK=O%Flags=R%Ops=)

T5(Resp=Y%DF=N%W=0%ACK=S++%Flags=AR%Ops=)

T6(Resp=N)

T7(Resp=Y%DF=N%W=0%ACK=S++%Flags=AR%Ops=)

PU(Resp=Y%DF=N%TOS=0%IPLEN=38%RIPTL=148%RID=E%RIPCK=F%UCK=E%ULEN=134%
DAT=E)

Interesting ports on 192.168.1.103:

(The 1666 ports scanned but not shown below are in state: closed.)

Port State Service

21/tcp open ftp

22/tcp open ssh

80/tcp open http

111/tcp open rpcbind

113/tcp open auth

3306/tcp open mysql

MAC Address: 00:09:7A:44:15:DB (Louis Design Labs.)

Device type: general purpose

Running: Linux 2.4.X|2.5.X

OS details: Linux 2.4.0 - 2.5.20

Uptime 0.265 days (since Sun Feb 19 18:44:17 2006)

Interesting ports on 192.168.1.104:

```
(The 1669 ports scanned but not shown below are in state: closed.)

Port State Service

22/tcp open ssh

111/tcp open rpcbind

5060/tcp open sip

Device type: general purpose

Running: Linux 2.4.X|2.5.X|2.6.X

OS details: Linux 2.5.25 - 2.6.8 or Gentoo 1.2 Linux 2.4.19 rc1-rc7, Linux

2.6.3 - 2.6.10

Uptime 0.261 days (since Sun Feb 19 18:49:06 2006)

Nmap finished: 84 IP addresses (14 hosts up) scanned in 77.843 seconds.
```

Nmap is one of several tools that analyze TCP, UDP, and ICMP protocol requests for OS and firmware identification. Other tools include Xprobe2 and Queso.

Step 11: Banner Grabbing

Banner grabbing, also known as banner scraping, is a method of connecting to a port on a remote target to determine further information about the associated services running on that specific port. This is one of the most popular attacks used to determine VoIP applications and hardware. Attackers can use this method to gather information on specific service types and versions.

The command-line tool Netcat is used for banner grabbing, as shown in the following example:

```
nc 192.168.1.103 80

GET / HTTP/1.1

HTTP/1.1 400 Bad Request

Date: Sun, 05 Mar 2006 22:15:40 GMT

Server: Apache/2.0.46 (CentOS)

Content-Length: 309

Connection: close

Content-Type: text/html; charset=iso-8859-1

<!DOCTYPE HTML PUBLIC "-//IETF//DTD HTML 2.0//EN">

<html><head>

<title>400 Bad Request</title>

</head><body>

<h1>Bad Request</h1>

<p>Your browser sent a request that this server could not
understand.<br />

</p>

<hr />

<address>Apache/2.0.46 (CentOS) Server at 192.168.1.103 Port 80</address>

</body></html>
```

The above error response shows that the Web server is running Apache HTTPd version 2.0.46 on the CentOS operating system.

Information about the SIP service connected to a port can be manually identified by using the OPTIONS method as follows:

```
nc 192.168.1.104 5060

OPTIONS sip:test@192.168.1.104 SIP/2.0

Via: SIP/2.0/TCP 192.168.1.120;branch=4ivBcVj5ZnPYgb

To: alice <sip:test@192.168.1.104>

Content-Length: 0

SIP/2.0 404 Not Found

Via: SIP/2.0/TCP
192.168.1.120;branch=4ivBcVj5ZnPYgb;received=192.168.1.103

To: alice
<sip:test@192.168.1.104>;tag=b27e1a1d33761e85846fc98f5f3a7e58.0503

Server: Sip EXpress router (0.9.6 (i386/linux))

Content-Length: 0

Warning: 392 192.168.1.104:5060 "Noisy feedback tells: pid=29801 req _
src _

ip=192.168.1.120 req _ src _ port=32773 in _ uri=sip:test@192.168.1.104 out _

uri=sip:test@192.168.1.104 via _ cnt==1"
```

Smap is an SIP scanning and fingerprinting tool that analyzes SIP message responses to find out the type of device it is probing. The following example shows automated banner grabbing using Smap:

```
smap -o 89.53.17.208/29

smap 0.4.0-cvs <hscholz@raisdorf.net> http://www.wormulon.net/

Host 89.53.17.208:5060: (ICMP OK) SIP timeout

Host 89.53.17.209:5060: (ICMP OK) SIP enabled

AVM FRITZ!Box Fon Series firmware: 14.03.(89|90) (Oct 28 2005)

Host 89.53.17.210:5060: (ICMP timeout) SIP timeout

Host 89.53.17.211:5060: (ICMP OK) SIP enabled

AVM FRITZ!Box Fon Series firmware: 14.03.(89|90) (Oct 28 2005)

Host 89.53.17.212:5060: (ICMP OK) SIP enabled

AVM FRITZ!Box Fon Series firmware: 14.03.(89|90) (Oct 28 2005)

Host 89.53.17.213:5060: (ICMP timeout) SIP enabled

Siemens SX541 (firmware 1.67)

Host 89.53.17.214:5060: (ICMP OK) SIP enabled

AVM FRITZ!Box Fon Series firmware: 14.03.(89|90) (Oct 28 2005)

Host 89.53.17.215:5060: (ICMP OK) SIP enabled

AVM FRITZ!Box Fon ata 11.03.45

8 hosts scanned, 6 ICMP reachable, 6 SIP enabled$
```

Step 12: SIP User/Extension Enumeration

In order to launch attacks, attackers may need valid usernames or extensions of SIP phones, registration servers, and proxy servers. They may attempt to discover valid extensions using a brute-force wardialer.

Other enumeration methods involve observing the error messages returned by the three SIP methods: REGISTER, OPTIONS, and INVITE. Although all servers and user agents may not support all three methods, even one or two of them can provide vital information.

The chief target of the hacker is the SIP proxy or registrar because they are the common places to extract user registration and presence. Determining an SIP phone's IP address may allow an attacker to also uncover its extension.

Methods of enumeration include the following:

- REGISTER username enumeration

- INVITE username enumeration

- OPTIONS username enumeration

- Automated OPTIONS scanning with sipsak

- Automated REGISTER, INVITE, and OPTIONS scanning with SIPSCAN against an SIP server

- Automated OPTIONS scanning using SIPSCAN against SIP phones

Step 13: Automated OPTIONS Scanning with Sipsak

Sipsak is a command-line tool used for OPTIONS scanning, which is useful for stress testing and diagnosing SIP service issues. By default, sipsak only supports OPTIONS requests. The following example using sipsak shows an attempt to probe an SIP Express Router proxy server with the valid extension 506:

```
sipsak -vv -s sip:506@192.168.1.104

New message with Via-Line:

OPTIONS sip:506@192.168.1.104 SIP/2.0

Via: SIP/2.0/UDP asterisk1.local:32874;rport

From: sip:sipsak@asterisk1.local:32874;tag=702e3179

To: sip:506@192.168.1.104

Call-ID: 1882075513@asterisk1.local

CSeq: 1 OPTIONS

Contact: sip:sipsak@asterisk1.local:32874

Content-Length: 0

Max-Forwards: 70

User-Agent: sipsak 0.8.11

Accept: text/plain

** request **

OPTIONS sip:506@192.168.1.104 SIP/2.0

Via: SIP/2.0/UDP asterisk1.local:32874;rport

From: sip:sipsak@asterisk1.local:32874;tag=702e3179

To: sip:506@192.168.1.104

Call-ID: 1882075513@asterisk1.local

CSeq: 1 OPTIONS

Contact: sip:sipsak@asterisk1.local:32874

Content-Length: 0

Max-Forwards: 70

User-Agent: sipsak 0.8.11
```

```
Accept: text/plain
message received:
SIP/2.0 200 Ok
Via: SIP/2.0/UDP asterisk1.local:32874;received=192.168.1.103;rport=32874
From: sip:sipsak@asterisk1.local:32874;tag=702e3179
To: <sip:506@192.168.1.104>;tag=644497335
Contact: <sip:506@192.168.1.56:5060>
Call-ID: 1882075513@asterisk1.local
Allow: INVITE,ACK,BYE,CANCEL,OPTIONS,NOTIFY
CSeq: 1 OPTIONS
Server: X-Lite release 1105x
Content-Length: 0
** reply received after 5.479 ms **
SIP/2.0 200 Ok
final received
```

The following is an attempt to probe the server using the invalid extension *thisisthecanary*:

```
sipsak -vv -s sip:thisisthecanary@192.168.1.104
New message with Via-Line:
OPTIONS sip:thisisthecanary@192.168.1.104 SIP/2.0
Via: SIP/2.0/UDP asterisk1.local:32876;rport
From: sip:sipsak@asterisk1.local:32876;tag=1aeccc21
To: sip:thisisthecanary@192.168.1.104
Call-ID: 451726369@asterisk1.local
CSeq: 1 OPTIONS
Contact: sip:sipsak@asterisk1.local:32876
Content-Length: 0
Max-Forwards: 70
User-Agent: sipsak 0.8.11
Accept: text/plain
** request **
OPTIONS sip:thisisthecanary@192.168.1.104 SIP/2.0
Via: SIP/2.0/UDP asterisk1.local:32876;rport
From: sip:sipsak@asterisk1.local:32876;tag=1aeccc21
To: sip:thisisthecanary@192.168.1.104
Call-ID: 451726369@asterisk1.local
CSeq: 1 OPTIONS
Contact: sip:sipsak@asterisk1.local:32876
Content-Length: 0
```

```
Max-Forwards: 70

User-Agent: sipsak 0.8.11

Accept: text/plain

message received:

SIP/2.0 404 Not Found

Via: SIP/2.0/UDP asterisk1.local:32876;rport=32876;received=192.168.1.103

From: sip:sipsak@asterisk1.local:32876;tag=1aeccc21

To:
sip:thisisthecanary@192.168.1.104;tag=b27e1a1d33761e85846fc98f5f3a7e58.9
543

Call-ID: 451726369@asterisk1.local

CSeq: 1 OPTIONS

Server: Sip EXpress router (0.9.6 (i386/linux))

Content-Length: 0

Warning: 392 192.168.1.104:5060 "Noisy feedback tells: pid=29782

req_src_ip=192.168.1.103 req_src_port=32876

in_uri=sip:thisisacanary@192.168.1.104

out_uri=sip:thisisacanary@192.168.1.104 via_cnt==1"

** reply received after 0.562 ms **

SIP/2.0 404 Not Found

final received
```

Sipsak can be scripted to iterate a list of usernames and then parse the output afterward in order to identify live extensions as follows:

```perl
#!/usr/local/bin/perl

@usernames =

(500,501,505,503,504,505,506,507,508,509,510,511,512,513,514,515);

foreach $key (@usernames) {

system("sipsak -vv -s sip:$key\@192.168.1.104 >\> sipsak_output.txt")

}
```

Step 14: Automated REGISTER, INVITE, and OPTIONS Scanning with SIPSCAN Against an SIP Server

Because the sipsak tool requires complicated reconfiguration to scan with INVITE and REGISTER requests, penetration testers can use the graphical SIP username/extension enumeration tool called SIPSCAN for these requests. SIPSCAN returns the live SIP extensions and users that it locates. By default, it brute-force-attacks a list of usernames (users.txt), which the tester can customize. For example, say the users.txt file includes the following:

```
thisisthecanary

test

echo

admin

dave
```

101
102
103
104
104
105
106
107
108
110
201
202
203
204
204
205
206
207
208
210
401
402
403
404
404
405
406
407
408
410
501
502
503
504
504
505
506
507
508

It is important that the first username in this list is invalid, because SIPSCAN uses it to baseline an invalid SIP response. The following is an example of the results from a REGISTER scanning attempt using SIPSCAN against an Asterisk server:

```
SIPSCAN Results:

Scan started Mon Mar 6 01:19:10 2006

Target SIP Server: 192.168.1.103:5060 UDP

Domain: 192.168.1.103

1>\>Found a live extension/user at 201@192.168.1.103

with SIP response code(s): REGISTER:401

2>\>Found a live extension/user at 202@192.168.1.103

with SIP response code(s): REGISTER:401

3>\>Found a live extension/user at 203@192.168.1.103

with SIP response code(s): REGISTER:401

4>\>Found a live extension/user at 204@192.168.1.103

with SIP response code(s): REGISTER:401

5>\>Found a live extension/user at 204@192.168.1.103

with SIP response code(s): REGISTER:401

6>\>Found a live extension/user at 205@192.168.1.103

with SIP response code(s): REGISTER:401

7>\>Found a live extension/user at 207@192.168.1.103

with SIP response code(s): REGISTER:401
```

Here, the REGISTER scan is successful in searching out the valid extensions. The following are the results of an OPTIONS scan:

```
SIPSCAN Results:

Scan started Mon Mar 6 01:28:16 2006

Target SIP Server: 192.168.1.103:5060 UDP

Domain: 192.168.1.103
```

There is no result, because all clients returned a 200 OK SIP response, making it impossible to differentiate between valid extensions and invalid extensions. SIPSCAN can combine the results from all scanning methods and display merged output as follows:

```
SIPSCAN Results:

Scan started Mon Mar 6 01:35:10 2006

Target SIP Server: 192.168.1.103:5060 UDP

Domain: 192.168.1.103

1>\>Found a live extension/user at 201@192.168.1.103

with SIP response code(s): REGISTER:401 OPTIONS: 200

2>\>Found a live extension/user at 202@192.168.1.103

with SIP response code(s): REGISTER:401 OPTIONS: 200

3>\>Found a live extension/user at 203@192.168.1.103

with SIP response code(s): REGISTER:401 OPTIONS: 200
```

```
4>\>Found a live extension/user at 204@192.168.1.103

with SIP response code(s): REGISTER:401 OPTIONS: 200

5>\>Found a live extension/user at 204@192.168.1.103

with SIP response code(s): REGISTER:401 OPTIONS: 200

6>\>Found a live extension/user at 205@192.168.1.103

with SIP response code(s): REGISTER:401 OPTIONS: 200

7>\>Found a live extension/user at 207@192.168.1.103

with SIP response code(s): REGISTER:401 OPTIONS: 200
```

Step 15: Enumerating TFTP Servers

Many VoIP phones use a Trivial File Transfer Protocol (TFTP) server to download configuration settings each time they power on. TFTP does not require any authentication to upload or download files, so one of the easiest ways for a hacker to compromise a VoIP network is to attack the TFTP servers.

TFTP servers usually use UDP port 69. The following shows an Nmap scan for this port:

```
Starting nmap 3.81 (http://www.insecure.org/nmap/) at 2006-03-07 01:56 CST

Interesting ports on 192.168.1.21:

PORT STATE SERVICE

69/udp closed tftp

MAC Address: 00:04:13:24:23:8D (Snom Technology AG)

Interesting ports on 192.168.1.22:

PORT STATE SERVICE

69/udp open|filtered tftp

MAC Address: 00:0F:34:11:80:45 (Cisco Systems)

Interesting ports on 192.168.1.23:

PORT STATE SERVICE

69/udp closed tftp

MAC Address: 00:15:62:86:BA:3E (Unknown)

Interesting ports on 192.168.1.24:

PORT STATE SERVICE

69/udp closed tftp

MAC Address: 00:0E:08:DA:DA:17 (Sipura Technology)

Interesting ports on 192.168.1.25:

PORT STATE SERVICE

69/udp closed tftp

MAC Address: 00:0B:82:06:4D:37 (Grandstream Networks)

Interesting ports on 192.168.1.27:

PORT STATE SERVICE

69/udp open|filtered tftp
```

```
MAC Address: 00:04:F2:03:15:46 (Circa Communications)

Interesting ports on 192.168.1.51:

PORT STATE SERVICE

69/udp closed tftp

MAC Address: 00:04:13:23:34:95 (Snom Technology AG)

Interesting ports on 192.168.1.53:

PORT STATE SERVICE

69/udp closed tftp

MAC Address: 00:04:0D:50:40:B0 (Avaya)

Interesting ports on 192.168.1.54:

PORT STATE SERVICE

69/udp closed tftp

MAC Address: 00:0E:08:DA:24:AE (Sipura Technology)

Interesting ports on 192.168.1.55:

PORT STATE SERVICE

69/udp open|filtered tftp

MAC Address: 00:E0:11:03:03:97 (Uniden SAN Diego R&D Center)

Interesting ports on 192.168.1.57:

PORT STATE SERVICE

69/udp open|filtered tftp

MAC Address: 00:01:E1:02:C8:DB (Kinpo Electronics)

Interesting ports on 192.168.1.103:

PORT STATE SERVICE

69/udp open|filtered tftp

MAC Address: 00:09:7A:44:15:DB (Louis Design Labs.)

Interesting ports on domain2 (192.168.1.104):

PORT STATE SERVICE

69/udp closed tftp
```

Here, a TFTP server is on 192.168.1.103. Banner-grabbing tools can determine the specific TFTP service running on this server.

TFTP does not have a method for a directory listing. Attackers must know the specific filenames to download, so they may use brute-force methods to attempt to download all files on the server. The following example uses the TFTPbrute.pl script to download all of the files named in brutefile.txt:

perl tftpbrute.pl 192.168.1.103 brutefile.txt 100

```
tftpbrute.pl, V 0.1

TFTP file word database: brutefile.txt

TFTP server 192.168.1.103

Max processes 100

Processes are: 1

Processes are: 2
```

```
Processes are: 3

Processes are: 4

Processes are: 5

Processes are: 6

Processes are: 7

Processes are: 8

Processes are: 9

Processes are: 10

Processes are: 11

Processes are: 12

*** Found TFTP server remote filename : sip.cfg

*** Found TFTP server remote filename : 46xxsettings.txt

Processes are: 13

Processes are: 14

*** Found TFTP server remote filename : sip _ 4602D02A.txt

*** Found TFTP server remote filename : XMLDefault.cnf.xml

*** Found TFTP server remote filename : SipDefault.cnf

*** Found TFTP server remote filename : SEP001562EA69E8.cnf
```

An attacker can download these files and search further for more information, just as in the following example:

```
tftp 192.168.1.103

tftp> get SEP001562EA69E8.cnf

cat SEP001562EA69E8.cnf

# SIP Configuration Generic File (start)

# Line 1 Settings

line1 _ name: "502" ; Line 1 Extension\User ID

line1 _ displayname: "502" ; Line 1 Display Name

line1 _ authname: "502" ; Line 1 Registration Authentication

line1 _ password: "1234" ; Line 1 Registration Password

# Line 2 Settings

line2 _ name: "" ; Line 2 Extension\User ID

line2 _ displayname: "" ; Line 2 Display Name

line2 _ authname: "UNPROVISIONED" ; Line 2 Registration Authentication

line2 _ password: "UNPROVISIONED" ; Line 2 Registration Password

# Line 3 Settings

line3 _ name: "" ; Line 3 Extension\User ID

line3 _ displayname: "" ; Line 3 Display Name

line3 _ authname: "UNPROVISIONED" ; Line 3 Registration Authentication

line3 _ password: "UNPROVISIONED" ; Line 3 Registration Password
```

```
# Line 4 Settings
line4_name: "" ; Line 4 Extension\User ID
line4_displayname: "" ; Line 4 Display Name
line4_authname: "UNPROVISIONED" ; Line 4 Registration Authentication
line4_password: "UNPROVISIONED" ; Line 4 Registration Password
# Line 5 Settings
line5_name: "" ; Line 5 Extension\User ID
line5_displayname: "" ; Line 5 Display Name
line5_authname: "UNPROVISIONED" ; Line 5 Registration Authentication
line5_password: "UNPROVISIONED" ; Line 5 Registration Password
# Line 6 Settings
line6_name: "" ; Line 6 Extension\User ID
line6_displayname: "" ; Line 6 Display Name
line6_authname: "UNPROVISIONED" ; Line 6 Registration Authentication
line6_password: "UNPROVISIONED" ; Line 6 Registration Password
# NAT/Firewall Traversal
nat_address: ""
VoIP_control_port: "5060"
start_media_port: "16384"
end_media_port: "32766"
# Phone Label (Text desired to be displayed in upper right corner)
phone_label: "cisco 7960" ; Has no effect on SIP messaging
# Time Zone phone will reside in
time_zone: EST
# Phone prompt/password for telnet/console session
phone_prompt: "Cisco7960" ; Telnet/Console Prompt
phone_password: "abc" ; Telnet/Console Password
# SIP Configuration Generic File (stop)
```

Step 16: SNMP Enumeration

In many VoIP devices, SNMP is an insecure protocol listening on port 162. Nmap can be used to check if any devices are using SNMP by checking port 162 using the -p option, as follows:

```
nmap -sU 192.168.1.1-254 -p 162
```

This can provide configuration information, including vendor, OS, MAC address, and ports of UDP services.

The snmpwalk tool can enumerate the configuration settings on phones as shown in the following example:

```
snmpwalk -c public -v 1 192.168.1.53
SNMPv2-MIB::sysDescr.0 = STRING: VxWorks SNMPv1/v2c Agent
SNMPv2-MIB::sysObjectID.0 = OID: SNMPv2-SMI::enterprises.6889.1.69.1.5
SNMPv2-MIB::sysUpTime.0 = Timeticks: (207512) 0:34:35.12
```

```
SNMPv2-MIB::sysContact.0 = STRING: Wind River Systems

SNMPv2-MIB::sysName.0 = STRING: AV

SNMPv2-MIB::sysLocation.0 = STRING: Planet Earth

SNMPv2-MIB::sysServices.0 = INTEGER: 79

IF-MIB::ifNumber.0 = INTEGER: 2

IF-MIB::ifIndex.1 = INTEGER: 1

IF-MIB::ifIndex.2 = INTEGER: 2

IF-MIB::ifDescr.1 = STRING: Avaya0

IF-MIB::ifDescr.2 = STRING: lo0

IF-MIB::ifType.1 = INTEGER: ethernetCsmacd(6)

IF-MIB::ifType.2 = INTEGER: softwareLoopback(24)

IF-MIB::ifMtu.1 = INTEGER: 1500

IF-MIB::ifMtu.2 = INTEGER: 32768

IF-MIB::ifSpeed.1 = Gauge32: 10000000

IF-MIB::ifSpeed.2 = Gauge32: 0

IF-MIB::ifPhysAddress.1 = STRING: 0:4:d:50:40:b0

IF-MIB::ifPhysAddress.2 = STRING:

IF-MIB::ifAdminStatus.1 = INTEGER: up(1)

IF-MIB::ifAdminStatus.2 = INTEGER: up(1)

IF-MIB::ifOperStatus.1 = INTEGER: up(1)

IF-MIB::ifOperStatus.2 = INTEGER: up(1)

IF-MIB::ifLastChange.1 = Timeticks: (0) 0:00:00.00

IF-MIB::ifLastChange.2 = Timeticks: (0) 0:00:00.00

IF-MIB::ifInOctets.1 = Counter32: 0

IF-MIB::ifInOctets.2 = Counter32: 0

IF-MIB::ifInUcastPkts.1 = Counter32: 736

IF-MIB::ifInUcastPkts.2 = Counter32: 106

IF-MIB::ifInNUcastPkts.1 = Counter32: 99

IF-MIB::ifInNUcastPkts.2 = Counter32: 0

IF-MIB::ifInDiscards.1 = Counter32: 0

IF-MIB::ifInDiscards.2 = Counter32: 0

IF-MIB::ifInErrors.1 = Counter32: 0

IF-MIB::ifInErrors.2 = Counter32: 0

IF-MIB::ifInUnknownProtos.1 = Counter32: 0

IF-MIB::ifInUnknownProtos.2 = Counter32: 0

IF-MIB::ifOutOctets.1 = Counter32: 0

IF-MIB::ifOutOctets.2 = Counter32: 0

IF-MIB::ifOutUcastPkts.1 = Counter32: 742
```

```
IF-MIB::ifOutUcastPkts.2 = Counter32: 106

IF-MIB::ifOutNUcastPkts.1 = Counter32: 4

IF-MIB::ifOutNUcastPkts.2 = Counter32: 0

IF-MIB::ifOutDiscards.1 = Counter32: 0

IF-MIB::ifOutDiscards.2 = Counter32: 0

IF-MIB::ifOutErrors.1 = Counter32: 0

IF-MIB::ifOutErrors.2 = Counter32: 0

IF-MIB::ifOutQLen.1 = Gauge32: 0

IF-MIB::ifOutQLen.2 = Gauge32: 0

IF-MIB::ifSpecific.1 = OID: SNMPv2-SMI::zeroDotZero

IF-MIB::ifSpecific.2 = OID: SNMPv2-SMI::zeroDotZero

IP-MIB::ipForwarding.0 = INTEGER: forwarding(1)

IP-MIB::ipDefaultTTL.0 = INTEGER: 64

IP-MIB::ipInReceives.0 = Counter32: 864

IP-MIB::ipInHdrErrors.0 = Counter32: 0

IP-MIB::ipInAddrErrors.0 = Counter32: 0

IP-MIB::ipForwDatagrams.0 = Counter32: 0

IP-MIB::ipInUnknownProtos.0 = Counter32: 1

IP-MIB::ipInDiscards.0 = Counter32: 0

IP-MIB::ipInDelivers.0 = Counter32: 869

IP-MIB::ipOutRequests.0 = Counter32: 857

IP-MIB::ipOutDiscards.0 = Counter32: 0

IP-MIB::ipOutNoRoutes.0 = Counter32: 0

IP-MIB::ipReasmTimeout.0 = INTEGER: 60

IP-MIB::ipReasmReqds.0 = Counter32: 0

IP-MIB::ipReasmOKs.0 = Counter32: 0

IP-MIB::ipReasmFails.0 = Counter32: 0

IP-MIB::ipFragOKs.0 = Counter32: 0

IP-MIB::ipFragFails.0 = Counter32: 0

IP-MIB::ipFragCreates.0 = Counter32: 0

IP-MIB::ipAdEntAddr.127.0.0.1 = IpAddress: 127.0.0.1

IP-MIB::ipAdEntAddr.192.168.1.53 = IpAddress: 192.168.1.53

IP-MIB::ipAdEntIfIndex.127.0.0.1 = INTEGER: 2

IP-MIB::ipAdEntIfIndex.192.168.1.53 = INTEGER: 1

IP-MIB::ipAdEntNetMask.127.0.0.1 = IpAddress: 255.0.0.0

IP-MIB::ipAdEntNetMask.192.168.1.53 = IpAddress: 255.255.255.0

IP-MIB::ipAdEntBcastAddr.127.0.0.1 = INTEGER: 1

IP-MIB::ipAdEntBcastAddr.192.168.1.53 = INTEGER: 1
```

```
IP-MIB::ipAdEntReasmMaxSize.127.0.0.1 = INTEGER: 65535

IP-MIB::ipAdEntReasmMaxSize.192.168.1.53 = INTEGER: 65535

RFC1213-MIB::ipRouteDest.0.0.0.0 = IpAddress: 0.0.0.0

RFC1213-MIB::ipRouteDest.24.93.41.125 = IpAddress: 24.93.41.125

RFC1213-MIB::ipRouteDest.127.0.0.1 = IpAddress: 127.0.0.1

RFC1213-MIB::ipRouteDest.192.168.1.0 = IpAddress: 192.168.1.0

RFC1213-MIB::ipRouteIfIndex.0.0.0.0 = INTEGER: 1

RFC1213-MIB::ipRouteIfIndex.24.93.41.125 = INTEGER: 1

RFC1213-MIB::ipRouteIfIndex.127.0.0.1 = INTEGER: 2

RFC1213-MIB::ipRouteIfIndex.192.168.1.0 = INTEGER: 1

RFC1213-MIB::ipRouteMetric1.0.0.0.0 = INTEGER: 1

RFC1213-MIB::ipRouteMetric1.24.93.41.125 = INTEGER: 1

RFC1213-MIB::ipRouteMetric1.127.0.0.1 = INTEGER: 0

RFC1213-MIB::ipRouteMetric1.192.168.1.0 = INTEGER: 0

RFC1213-MIB::ipRouteMetric2.0.0.0.0 = INTEGER: -1

RFC1213-MIB::ipRouteMetric2.24.93.41.125 = INTEGER: -1

RFC1213-MIB::ipRouteMetric2.127.0.0.1 = INTEGER: -1

RFC1213-MIB::ipRouteMetric2.192.168.1.0 = INTEGER: -1

RFC1213-MIB::ipRouteMetric3.0.0.0.0 = INTEGER: -1

RFC1213-MIB::ipRouteMetric3.24.93.41.125 = INTEGER: -1

RFC1213-MIB::ipRouteMetric3.127.0.0.1 = INTEGER: -1

RFC1213-MIB::ipRouteMetric3.192.168.1.0 = INTEGER: -1

RFC1213-MIB::ipRouteMetric4.0.0.0.0 = INTEGER: -1

RFC1213-MIB::ipRouteMetric4.24.93.41.125 = INTEGER: -1

RFC1213-MIB::ipRouteMetric4.127.0.0.1 = INTEGER: -1

RFC1213-MIB::ipRouteMetric4.192.168.1.0 = INTEGER: -1

RFC1213-MIB::ipRouteNextHop.0.0.0.0 = IpAddress: 192.168.1.1

RFC1213-MIB::ipRouteNextHop.24.93.41.125 = IpAddress: 192.168.1.1

RFC1213-MIB::ipRouteNextHop.127.0.0.1 = IpAddress: 127.0.0.1

RFC1213-MIB::ipRouteNextHop.192.168.1.0 = IpAddress: 192.168.1.53

RFC1213-MIB::ipRouteType.0.0.0.0 = INTEGER: indirect(4)

RFC1213-MIB::ipRouteType.24.93.41.125 = INTEGER: indirect(4)

RFC1213-MIB::ipRouteType.127.0.0.1 = INTEGER: direct(3)

RFC1213-MIB::ipRouteType.192.168.1.0 = INTEGER: direct(3)

RFC1213-MIB::ipRouteProto.0.0.0.0 = INTEGER: other(1)

RFC1213-MIB::ipRouteProto.24.93.41.125 = INTEGER: local(2)

RFC1213-MIB::ipRouteProto.127.0.0.1 = INTEGER: local(2)

RFC1213-MIB::ipRouteProto.192.168.1.0 = INTEGER: local(2)
```

```
RFC1213-MIB::ipRouteAge.0.0.0.0 = INTEGER: 2067

RFC1213-MIB::ipRouteAge.24.93.41.125 = INTEGER: 2025

RFC1213-MIB::ipRouteAge.127.0.0.1 = INTEGER: 2079

RFC1213-MIB::ipRouteAge.192.168.1.0 = INTEGER: 2068

RFC1213-MIB::ipRouteMask.0.0.0.0 = IpAddress: 0.0.0.0

RFC1213-MIB::ipRouteMask.24.93.41.125 = IpAddress: 255.255.255.255

RFC1213-MIB::ipRouteMask.127.0.0.1 = IpAddress: 255.255.255.255

RFC1213-MIB::ipRouteMask.192.168.1.0 = IpAddress: 255.255.255.0

RFC1213-MIB::ipRouteMetric5.0.0.0.0 = INTEGER: -1

RFC1213-MIB::ipRouteMetric5.24.93.41.125 = INTEGER: -1

RFC1213-MIB::ipRouteMetric5.127.0.0.1 = INTEGER: -1

RFC1213-MIB::ipRouteMetric5.192.168.1.0 = INTEGER: -1

RFC1213-MIB::ipRouteInfo.0.0.0.0 = OID: SNMPv2-SMI::zeroDotZero

RFC1213-MIB::ipRouteInfo.24.93.41.125 = OID: SNMPv2-SMI::zeroDotZero

RFC1213-MIB::ipRouteInfo.127.0.0.1 = OID: SNMPv2-SMI::zeroDotZero

RFC1213-MIB::ipRouteInfo.192.168.1.0 = OID: SNMPv2-SMI::zeroDotZero

IP-MIB::ipNetToMediaIfIndex.1.192.168.1.104 = INTEGER: 1

IP-MIB::ipNetToMediaIfIndex.2.192.168.1.53 = INTEGER: 2

IP-MIB::ipNetToMediaPhysAddress.1.192.168.1.104 = STRING: 0:9:7a:44:17:d9

IP-MIB::ipNetToMediaPhysAddress.2.192.168.1.53 = STRING: 0:4:d:50:40:b0

IP-MIB::ipNetToMediaNetAddress.1.192.168.1.104 = IpAddress: 192.168.1.104

IP-MIB::ipNetToMediaNetAddress.2.192.168.1.53 = IpAddress: 192.168.1.53

IP-MIB::ipNetToMediaType.1.192.168.1.104 = INTEGER: dynamic(3)

IP-MIB::ipNetToMediaType.2.192.168.1.53 = INTEGER: static(4)

IP-MIB::ipRoutingDiscards.0 = Counter32: 0

IP-MIB::icmpInMsgs.0 = Counter32: 4

IP-MIB::icmpInErrors.0 = Counter32: 0

IP-MIB::icmpInDestUnreachs.0 = Counter32: 1

IP-MIB::icmpInTimeExcds.0 = Counter32: 0

IP-MIB::icmpInParmProbs.0 = Counter32: 0

IP-MIB::icmpInSrcQuenchs.0 = Counter32: 0

IP-MIB::icmpInRedirects.0 = Counter32: 0

IP-MIB::icmpInEchos.0 = Counter32: 3

IP-MIB::icmpInEchoReps.0 = Counter32: 0

IP-MIB::icmpInTimestamps.0 = Counter32: 0

IP-MIB::icmpInTimestampReps.0 = Counter32: 0

IP-MIB::icmpInAddrMasks.0 = Counter32: 0

IP-MIB::icmpInAddrMaskReps.0 = Counter32: 0
```

```
IP-MIB::icmpOutMsgs.0 = Counter32: 27

IP-MIB::icmpOutErrors.0 = Counter32: 24

IP-MIB::icmpOutDestUnreachs.0 = Counter32: 24

IP-MIB::icmpOutTimeExcds.0 = Counter32: 0

IP-MIB::icmpOutParmProbs.0 = Counter32: 0

IP-MIB::icmpOutSrcQuenchs.0 = Counter32: 0

IP-MIB::icmpOutRedirects.0 = Counter32: 0

IP-MIB::icmpOutEchos.0 = Counter32: 0

IP-MIB::icmpOutEchoReps.0 = Counter32: 3

IP-MIB::icmpOutTimestamps.0 = Counter32: 0

IP-MIB::icmpOutTimestampReps.0 = Counter32: 0

IP-MIB::icmpOutAddrMasks.0 = Counter32: 0

IP-MIB::icmpOutAddrMaskReps.0 = Counter32: 0

TCP-MIB::tcpRtoAlgorithm.0 = INTEGER: vanj(4)

TCP-MIB::tcpRtoMin.0 = INTEGER: 1000 milliseconds

TCP-MIB::tcpRtoMax.0 = INTEGER: 64000 milliseconds

TCP-MIB::tcpMaxConn.0 = INTEGER: -1

TCP-MIB::tcpActiveOpens.0 = Counter32: 6

TCP-MIB::tcpPassiveOpens.0 = Counter32: 4

TCP-MIB::tcpAttemptFails.0 = Counter32: 1

TCP-MIB::tcpEstabResets.0 = Counter32: 0

TCP-MIB::tcpCurrEstab.0 = Gauge32: 0

TCP-MIB::tcpInSegs.0 = Counter32: 96

TCP-MIB::tcpOutSegs.0 = Counter32: 99

TCP-MIB::tcpRetransSegs.0 = Counter32: 0

TCP-MIB::tcpInErrs.0 = Counter32: 0

TCP-MIB::tcpOutRsts.0 = Counter32: 0

UDP-MIB::udpInDatagrams.0 = Counter32: 890

UDP-MIB::udpNoPorts.0 = Counter32: 26

UDP-MIB::udpInErrors.0 = Counter32: 0

UDP-MIB::udpOutDatagrams.0 = Counter32: 855

UDP-MIB::udpLocalAddress.0.0.0.0.68 = IpAddress: 0.0.0.0

UDP-MIB::udpLocalAddress.0.0.0.0.161 = IpAddress: 0.0.0.0

UDP-MIB::udpLocalAddress.0.0.0.0.1031 = IpAddress: 0.0.0.0

UDP-MIB::udpLocalAddress.0.0.0.0.1033 = IpAddress: 0.0.0.0

UDP-MIB::udpLocalAddress.0.0.0.0.5060 = IpAddress: 0.0.0.0

UDP-MIB::udpLocalAddress.0.0.0.0.10000 = IpAddress: 0.0.0.0

UDP-MIB::udpLocalAddress.127.0.0.1.1032 = IpAddress: 127.0.0.1
```

```
UDP-MIB::udpLocalPort.0.0.0.0.68 = INTEGER: 68

UDP-MIB::udpLocalPort.0.0.0.0.161 = INTEGER: 161

UDP-MIB::udpLocalPort.0.0.0.0.1031 = INTEGER: 1031

UDP-MIB::udpLocalPort.0.0.0.0.1033 = INTEGER: 1033

UDP-MIB::udpLocalPort.0.0.0.0.5060 = INTEGER: 5060

UDP-MIB::udpLocalPort.0.0.0.0.10000 = INTEGER: 10000

UDP-MIB::udpLocalPort.127.0.0.1.1032 = INTEGER: 1032

SNMPv2-MIB::snmpInPkts.0 = Counter32: 799

SNMPv2-MIB::snmpOutPkts.0 = Counter32: 788

SNMPv2-MIB::snmpInBadVersions.0 = Counter32: 6

SNMPv2-MIB::snmpInBadCommunityNames.0 = Counter32: 6

SNMPv2-MIB::snmpInBadCommunityUses.0 = Counter32: 0

SNMPv2-MIB::snmpInASNParseErrs.0 = Counter32: 0

SNMPv2-MIB::snmpInTooBigs.0 = Counter32: 0

SNMPv2-MIB::snmpInNoSuchNames.0 = Counter32: 0

SNMPv2-MIB::snmpInBadValues.0 = Counter32: 0

SNMPv2-MIB::snmpInReadOnlys.0 = Counter32: 0

SNMPv2-MIB::snmpInGenErrs.0 = Counter32: 0

SNMPv2-MIB::snmpInTotalReqVars.0 = Counter32: 1067

SNMPv2-MIB::snmpInTotalSetVars.0 = Counter32: 0

SNMPv2-MIB::snmpInGetRequests.0 = Counter32: 22

SNMPv2-MIB::snmpInGetNexts.0 = Counter32: 749

SNMPv2-MIB::snmpInSetRequests.0 = Counter32: 0

SNMPv2-MIB::snmpInGetResponses.0 = Counter32: 0

SNMPv2-MIB::snmpInTraps.0 = Counter32: 0

SNMPv2-MIB::snmpOutTooBigs.0 = Counter32: 0

SNMPv2-MIB::snmpOutNoSuchNames.0 = Counter32: 0

SNMPv2-MIB::snmpOutBadValues.0 = Counter32: 0

SNMPv2-MIB::snmpOutGenErrs.0 = Counter32: 0

SNMPv2-MIB::snmpOutGetRequests.0 = Counter32: 0

SNMPv2-MIB::snmpOutGetNexts.0 = Counter32: 0

SNMPv2-MIB::snmpOutSetRequests.0 = Counter32: 0

SNMPv2-MIB::snmpOutGetResponses.0 = Counter32: 811

SNMPv2-MIB::snmpOutTraps.0 = Counter32: 1

SNMPv2-MIB::snmpEnableAuthenTraps.0 = INTEGER: disabled(2)

SNMPv2-MIB::snmpSilentDrops.0 = Counter32: 0

SNMPv2-MIB::snmpProxyDrops.0 = Counter32: 0

IF-MIB::ifName.1 = STRING:
```

```
IF-MIB::ifName.2 = STRING:

IF-MIB::ifInMulticastPkts.1 = Counter32: 0

IF-MIB::ifInMulticastPkts.2 = Counter32: 0

IF-MIB::ifInBroadcastPkts.1 = Counter32: 0

IF-MIB::ifInBroadcastPkts.2 = Counter32: 0

IF-MIB::ifOutMulticastPkts.1 = Counter32: 0

IF-MIB::ifOutMulticastPkts.2 = Counter32: 0

IF-MIB::ifOutBroadcastPkts.1 = Counter32: 0

IF-MIB::ifOutBroadcastPkts.2 = Counter32: 0

IF-MIB::ifLinkUpDownTrapEnable.1 = INTEGER: disabled(2)

IF-MIB::ifLinkUpDownTrapEnable.2 = INTEGER: disabled(2)

IF-MIB::ifHighSpeed.1 = Gauge32: 0

IF-MIB::ifHighSpeed.2 = Gauge32: 0

IF-MIB::ifPromiscuousMode.1 = INTEGER: false(2)

IF-MIB::ifPromiscuousMode.2 = INTEGER: false(2)

IF-MIB::ifConnectorPresent.1 = INTEGER: false(2)

IF-MIB::ifConnectorPresent.2 = INTEGER: false(2)

IF-MIB::ifAlias.1 = STRING:

IF-MIB::ifAlias.2 = STRING:

IF-MIB::ifCounterDiscontinuityTime.1 = Timeticks: (0) 0:00:00.00

IF-MIB::ifCounterDiscontinuityTime.2 = Timeticks: (0) 0:00:00.00

IF-MIB::ifStackStatus.0.1 = INTEGER: active(1)

IF-MIB::ifStackStatus.0.2 = INTEGER: active(1)

IF-MIB::ifStackStatus.1.0 = INTEGER: active(1)

IF-MIB::ifStackStatus.2.0 = INTEGER: active(1)

IF-MIB::ifRcvAddressStatus.1.". . . P@." = INTEGER: active(1)

IF-MIB::ifRcvAddressType.1.". . . P@." = INTEGER: nonVolatile(3)

IF-MIB::ifTableLastChange.0 = Timeticks: (0) 0:00:00.00

IF-MIB::ifStackLastChange.0 = Timeticks: (0) 0:00:00.00
```

Step 17: Sniffing TFTP Configuration File Transfers

Sniffing for TFTP configuration files passing through the VoIP network is as simple as examining any and all traffic on UDP port 69. This can be an easier way to find configuration filenames than just using brute force. The following example shows Tcpdump watching port 69:

```
tcpdump dst port 69

tcpdump: listening on eth0

02:43:18.899478 192.168.1.55.20000 > 192.168.1.103.tftp:

22 RRQ "unidencom.txt"

02:43:19.028863 192.168.1.55.19745 > 192.168.1.103.tftp:
```

```
31 RRQ "uniden00e011030397.txt"

02:43:37.878042 192.168.1.52.51154 > 192.168.1.103.tftp:

31 RRQ "CTLSEP001562EA69E8.tlv" [tos 0x10]

02:43:37.899329 192.168.1.52.51155 > 192.168.1.103.tftp:

32 RRQ "SEP001562EA69E8.cnf.xml" [tos 0x10]

02:43:37.919054 192.168.1.52.51156 > 192.168.1.103.tftp:

28 RRQ "SIP001562EA69E8.cnf" [tos 0x10]

02:43:37.968715 192.168.1.52.51157 > 192.168.1.103.tftp:

23 RRQ "SIPDefault.cnf" [tos 0x10]

02:43:38.017358 192.168.1.52.51158 > 192.168.1.103.tftp:

30 RRQ "./SIP001562EA69E8.cnf" [tos 0x10]

02:43:38.058998 192.168.1.52.51159 > 192.168.1.103.tftp:

27 RRQ "P0S3-07-5-00.loads" [tos 0x10]

02:43:56.777846 192.168.1.52.50642 > 192.168.1.103.tftp:

23 RRQ "SIPDefault.cnf" [tos 0x10]

02:43:56.943568 192.168.1.52.50643 > 192.168.1.103.tftp:

30 RRQ "./SIP001562EA69E8.cnf" [tos 0x10]

02:43:59.031713 192.168.1.52.50651 > 192.168.1.103.tftp:

21 RRQ "RINGLIST.DAT" [tos 0x10]

02:43:59.432906 192.168.1.52.50652 > 192.168.1.103.tftp:

21 RRQ "dialplan.xml" [tos 0x10]
```

Once the filenames are revealed, they can be downloaded directly from the TFTP server from any Linux or Windows command prompt as follows:

```
tftp 192.168.1.103

tftp> get SIP001562EA69E8.cnf
```

Step 18: Number Harvesting and Call Pattern Tracking

The easiest way to perform passive number harvesting in an SIP environment is to sniff all SIP traffic on UDP and TCP port 5060 and evaluate the *from:* and *to:* header fields. There are many tools available to perform such tests, such as the Wireshark packet sniffer.

The following example shows the VoIPong tool being used to log all calls to and from various IP addresses:

```
VoIPong -d4 -f

EnderUNIX VOIPONG Voice Over IP Sniffer starting...

Release 2.0-DEVEL, running on efe.dev.enderunix.org

[FreeBSD 4.10-STABLE FreeBSD 4.10-STABLE #0: Thu Dec i386]

(c) Murat Balaban http://www.enderunix.org/

19/11/04 13:32:10: EnderUNIX VOIPONG Voice Over IP Sniffer starting...

19/11/04 13:32:10: Release 2.0-DEVEL running on efe.dev.enderunix.org

[FreeBSD 4.10-STABLE FreeBSD 4.10-STABLE #0: Thu Dec i386].

(c) Murat Balaban http://www.enderunix.org/
```

```
[pid: 71647]

19/11/04 13:32:10: fxp0 has been opened in promisc mode,

data link: 14 (192.168.0.0/255.255.255.248)

19/11/04 13:32:10: [8434] VoIP call detected.

19/11/04 13:32:10: [8434] 10.0.0.49:49606 <--> 10.0.0.90:49604

19/11/04 13:32:10: [8434] Encoding: 0-PCMU-8KHz

19/11/04 13:38:37: [8434] maximum waiting time [10 sn] elapsed for this
call, call might have been ended.

19/11/04 13:38:37: .WAV file has been created successfully.

[output/20041119/session-enc0-PCMU-8KHz-10.0.0.49,49606-10.0.0.90,49604.wav]
```

VoIP Penetration Testing Tools

VoIP Sniffing Tools

AuthTool

AuthTool was developed to attempt to determine the password for every user of SIP messages. These username/password pairs can be used as input for a tool such as Registration Hijacker. SIP servers invoke MD5 authentication challenges to clients invoking these SIP requests:

- REGISTER
- INVITE
- OPTIONS

Before encountering an authorization header line, the tool expects to find at least one REGISTER, INVITE, or OPTIONS request line and at least one *From:* header line. The scan does not distinguish between SIP headers and SIP message bodies. If a line in a message body is encountered starting with any of the above keywords, the tool presumes that a SIP message header line has been found. SIP message fragments may cause the tool to perform poorly or even crash.

When an authorization header line is encountered, the tool attempts to extract the parameters required to recompute the MD5 digest that must also be present on that authorization line, and it then recomputes the digest as directed. It either employs a dictionary attack using the dictionary file specified on the command line, or it uses a single password specified on the command line. When it finds a successful password, the username, password, and URI are output to the result file. The tool completes when all SIP messages in the input file have been exhausted.

VoIPong

VoIPong detects all VoIP calls on a pipeline, and for those that are G711 encoded, it dumps actual conversations to separate WAV files. It supports SIP, H323, Cisco's Skinny Client Protocol, RTP, and RTCP, and runs on Solaris, Linux, and FreeBSD.

VoIPong is shown in Figure 3-2, and its features include the following:

- Simple, optimized, extendable fast code
- Depends on RTP/RTCP instead of signaling
- Detailed logging
- Powerful management console interface
- Easy installation and administration
- Easy debugging

```
Capture screen
efe:[voipong]# voipong -d4 -f EnderUNIX VOIPONG Voice Over IP
Sniffer starting... Release 2.0-DEVEL, running on
efe.dev.enderunix.org [FreeBSD 4.10-STABLE FreeBSD 4.10-STABLE #0:
Thu Dec i386] |(c) Murat Balaban http://www.enderunix.org/ 19/11/04
13:32:10: EnderUNIX VOIPONG Voice Over IP Sniffer starting...
19/11/04 13:32:10: Release 2.0-DEVEL running on
efe.dev.enderunix.org [FreeBSD 4.10-STABLE FreeBSD 4.10-STABLE #0:
Thu Dec i386]. (c) Murat Balaban http://www.enderunix.org/ [pid:
71647] 19/11/04 13:32:10: fxp0 has been opened in promisc mode,
data link: 14 (192.168.0.0/255.255.255.248) 19/11/04 13:32:10:
[8434] VoIP call detected. 19/11/04 13:32:10: [8434]
10.0.0.49:49606 <--> 10.0.0.90:49604 19/11/04 13:32:10: [8434]
Encoding: 0-PCMU-8KHz 19/11/04 13:38:37: [8434] maximum waiting
time [10 sn] elapsed for this call, call might have been ended.
19/11/04 13:38:37: .WAV file [output/20041119/session-enc0-PCMU-
8KHz-10.0.0.49,49606-10.0.0.90,49604.wav] has been created
successfully.
```

Figure 3-2   VoIPong dumps voice calls to WAV files.

vomit

The vomit utility converts a Cisco IP phone conversation into a WAV file. It is not a VoIP sniffer, so it requires a Tcpdump output file. vomit is distributed under a BSD license and is completely free for any use, including commercial use. vomit requires libevent (a library for asynchronous event notification) and libdnet or libnet. Its error utility works only for the G.711 VoIP infrastructure.

pcapsipdump

The pcapsipdump tool is used to dump SIP sessions, along with RTP traffic, if available. It uses the same output format as **tcpdump -w**, except it creates a unique file for each SIP session.

Netdude

Netdude is a GUI application that allows users to inspect and edit trace files without writing extensive code. It is a front end to the libnetdude packet manipulation library, which uses Tcpdump trace files and output to handle captured network traffic, illustrate networking issues, and test networking applications with canned traffic streams.

When more functionality is required, users can write plugins for Netdude. While these plugins are relatively simple to code, they have full access to the Netdude core. There are three kinds of plugins:

1. *Protocol plugins*: These provide a simple interface to the packets' protocol data. They can display packet data in any way. The protocol plugins that ship with Netdude use a tabular display of header fields, along with buttons that allow the user to inspect values and make modifications. Protocol plugins are registered in Netdude's protocol registry automatically, provided the user implements a set of callbacks. This set of callbacks provides support for both stateless and stateful protocols.

2. *Functionality plugins*: These plugins provide features that Netdude does not possess by default. These plugins can do just about anything, including correcting checksums, anonymizing data, and performing statistical analysis.

3. *Filter plugins*: Filter plugins are a variation of functionality plugins. Netdude provides a filtering framework, which filter plugins can use to register new filter code. Filters can be stateful (such as "drop all incomplete TCP connections") or stateless (such as "drop everything that does not go to or from TCP port 80").

Netdude is shown in Figure 3-3, and its features include the following:

- Edits traces of arbitrary size in a scalable fashion; Netdude never loads more than a configurable maximum number of packets into memory at any time

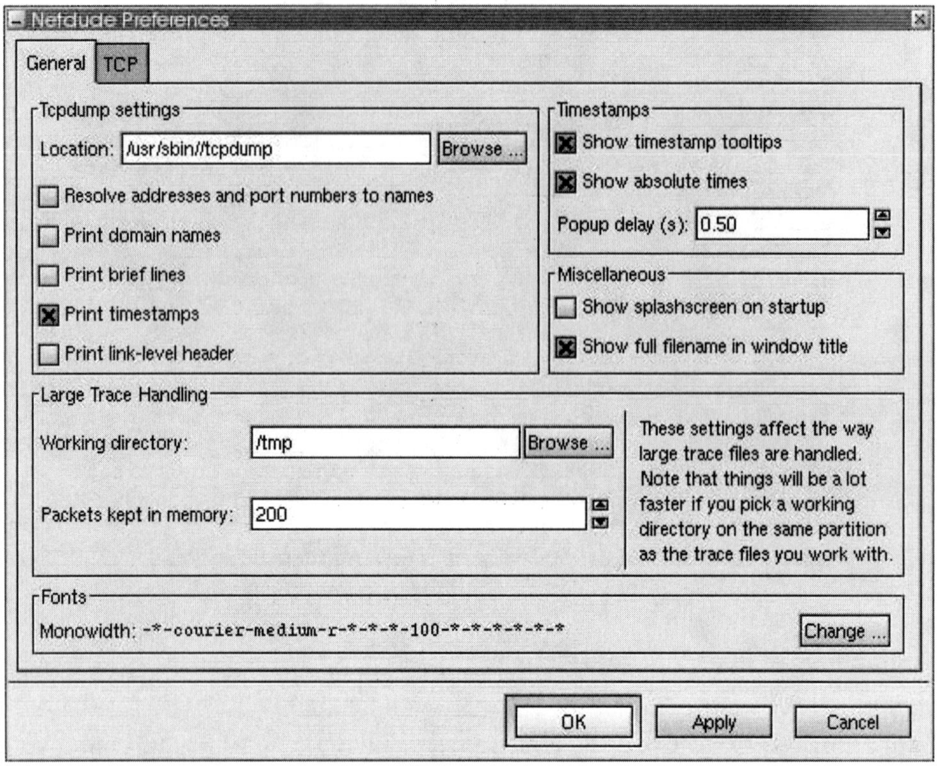

Source: http://netdude.sourceforge.net/screenshots/0.4/shot-5.gif. Accessed 2007.

Figure 3-3 Netdude is a front end to libnetdude, and users can write plugins to increase its utility.

- Edits multiple traces at the same time, making it easy to move packets from one trace to another
- Modifies every field in protocol headers, applied to individually selected packets, packets currently in memory, or all packets in the trace
- Filters packets by using filter plugins, using a BPF filter plugin that allows users to use the standard BPF filter language
- Inspects and edits raw packet content using Netdude's payload editor in either hex or ASCII mode
- Moves packets around, duplicates them, and removes them from traces
- Updates Tcpdump output instantly
- Uses the clipboard to select lines from Tcpdump output

Oreka

Oreka is a modular, cross-platform system for recording and retrieving audio streams from VoIP and sound devices. Metadata about the recordings can be stored in any mainstream database. Oreka includes the following services:

- OrkAudio
- OrkTrack
- OrkWeb

Oreka can retrieve recordings based on the following critiera:

- Time stamp
- Recording duration
- Direction (for a telephone call)
- Remote party (for a telephone call)
- Local party (for a telephone call)

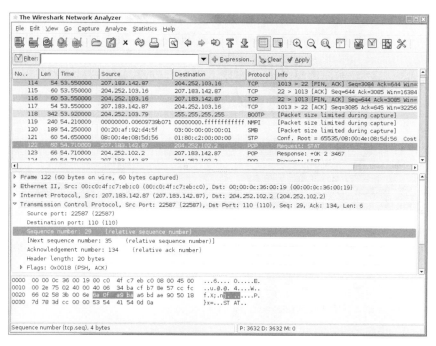

Figure 3-4   Wireshark is an industry-standard network protocol analyzer.

Oreka's features include:

- Records VoIP RTP sessions by passively listening to network packets, mixing both sides of a conversation together and logging each call as a separate audio file
- Records from a standard sound device with multiple simultaneous channels
- Open plug-in architecture, allowing the system to potentially record from any audio source
- Plug-in architecture for codecs or any other signal-processing filter
- Automatic audio segmentation to split long audio sources into separate audio files
- Captures from multiple network devices in parallel
- Captures from pcap trace files
- Voice activity detection
- A-Law, U-Law, and GSM 6.10 codecs supported as both wire and storage format
- Automatic transcoding from wire format to storage format
- Compatible with the following:
  - Lucent APX8000
  - Avaya S8500
  - Siemens HiPath
  - VocalData
  - Sylantro
  - Asterisk SIP channel

Wireshark

Wireshark is a widely used network protocol analyzer. It is shown in Figure 3-4, and its features include the following:

- Supports live capture and offline analysis
- Uses a standard three-pane packet browser

- Runs on Windows, Linux, OS X, Solaris, FreeBSD, NetBSD, and many others
- Captured network data can be browsed via a GUI, or via the TTY-mode TShark utility
- Powerful display filters
- Rich VoIP analysis
- Reads and writes many different capture file formats, including:
  - Tcpdump (libpcap)
  - Catapult DCT2000
  - Cisco Secure IDS iplog
  - Microsoft Network Monitor
  - NAI Sniffer (compressed and uncompressed)
  - Sniffer Pro
  - NetXray
  - Network Instruments Observer
  - Novell LANalyzer
  - RADCOM WAN/LAN Analyzer
  - Shomiti/Finisar Surveyor
  - Tektronix K12xx
  - Visual Networks Visual UpTime
  - WildPackets EtherPeek/TokenPeek/AiroPeek
- Captures files compressed with gzip can be decompressed on the fly
- Live data can be read from sources including:
  - Ethernet
  - IEEE 802.11
  - PPP/HDLC
  - ATM
  - Bluetooth
  - USB
  - Token Ring
  - Frame Relay
  - FDDI
- Decryption support for many protocols, including:
  - IPsec
  - ISAKMP
  - Kerberos
  - SSL/TLS
  - WEP
  - WPA/WPA2
- Supports hundreds of network protocols
- Coloring rules can be applied to the packet list
- Output can be exported to XML, PostScript, CSV, or text

rtpBreak

rtpBreak detects, reconstructs, and analyzes any RTP session over UDP. It works with SIP, H.323, SCCP, and any other signaling protocol. It does not require the presence of RTCP packets, works independently of the protocol in use, and supports wireless networks. rtpBreak is shown in Figure 3-5.

```
xenion@gollum:~/dev/rtpbreak-1.3$ cat logz/rtp.0.0.txt
RTP stream id: rtp.0.0
Packet source: iface  'wifi0'
First seen packet: 19/02/2008#09:49:29 (pcap time)
Stream peers: 192.168.0.30:2072 => 192.168.0.20:2074
RTP ssrc: 1695569992
RTP payload type: 0 (ITU-T G.711 PCMU)
Last seen packet: 19/02/2008#09:50:57 (pcap time)
Call length: 1m28s
Flushed packets: 2819
Lost packets: 106 (3.62%)
RTP payload length: 240 bytes (fixed)
xenion@gollum:~/dev/rtpbreak-1.3$ cat logz/rtp.0.1.txt
RTP stream id: rtp.0.1
Packet source: iface  'wifi0'
First seen packet: 19/02/2008#09:49:29 (pcap time)
Stream peers: 192.168.0.20:2074 => 192.168.0.30:2072
RTP ssrc: 112268413
RTP payload type: 0 (ITU-T G.711 PCMU)
Probable reverse RTP stream id: rtp.0.0
Last seen packet: 19/02/2008#09:50:57 (pcap time)
Call length: 1m28s
Flushed packets: 2800
Lost packets: 115 (3.95%)
RTP payload length: 240 bytes (fixed)
xenion@gollum:~/dev/rtpbreak-1.3$
```

Figure 3-5   rtpBreak is able to detect, reconstruct, and analyze RTP sessions.

VoIP Scanning and Enumeration Tools

SNScan

SNScan is a Windows-based SNMP detection utility that can quickly and accurately identify SNMP-enabled devices on a network. This helps a user find devices potentially vulnerable to SNMP-related security threats. It scans SNMP-specific ports (UDP ports 161, 193, 391, and 1993) and uses both standard and user-defined SNMP community names. SNScan is shown in Figure 3-6.

Netcat

Netcat is networking utility that reads and writes data across network connections using the TCP/IP protocol. It is designed to work reliably when used either directly or driven by other programs and scripts. Netcat is distributed freely under a GNU General Public License (GPL).

Netcat's features include the following:

- Supports outbound and inbound connections, TCP or UDP, to or from any ports

- Tunneling mode allows special tunneling such as UDP to TCP, with the possibility of specifying all network parameters (source port/interface, listening port/interface, and the remote host allowed to connect to the tunnel)

- Built-in port-scanning capabilities, with randomizer

- Advanced usage options, such as buffered send mode (one line every *N* seconds) and hex dump (to stderr or to a specified file) of transmitted and received data

- Optional RFC854 telnet codes parser and responder

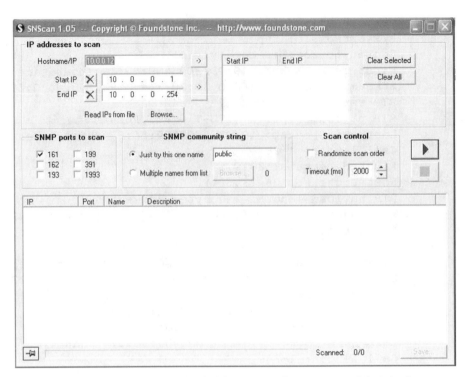

Figure 3-6   SNScan is a fast and reliable scanner for SNMP-enabled devices.

```
$ ./smap -l 89.53.17.214

smap 0.4.0-cvs <hscholz@raisdorf.net> http://www.wormulon.net/

NOTICE: test_allow: "Allow: INVITE, ACK, OPTIONS, CANCEL, BYE, UPDATE, PRACK, INFO,
SUBSCRIBE, NOTIFY, REFER, MESSAGE"
Host 89.53.17.214:5060: (ICMP OK) SIP enabled
best guess (71% sure) fingerprint:
AVM FRITZ!Box Fon Series firmware: 14.03.(89|90) (Oct 28 2005)

FINGERPRINT information:
newmethod=405
allow_class=2
supported_class=ignore
hoe_class=ignore
options=NR
brokenfromto=NR
prack=405
ping=NR
invite=406
headers found:
User-Agent: AVM FRITZ!Box Fon WLAN 7050 14.03.89 (3.01.03 tested by accredited T-Com
test lab) (Oct 28 2005)

1 host scanned, 1 ICMP reachable, 1 SIP enabled
$
```

Figure 3-7   Smap is used for locating and fingerprinting remote SIP devices.

Smap

Smap is a combination of the Nmap and sipsak tools that is useful for locating and fingerprinting remote SIP devices. Smap's learning mode is shown in Figure 3-7.

SIPSCAN

SIPSCAN uses the REGISTER, INVITE, and OPTIONS scanning methods, and only returns the live extensions or users that it finds. By default, SIPSCAN comes with a list of usernames (users.txt) to try. This list should be tailored to fit the specific testing environment. SIPSCAN is shown in Figure 3-8.

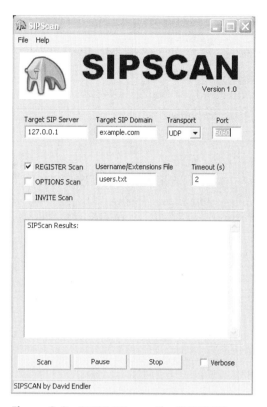

Figure 3-8   SIPSCAN uses the REGISTER, INVITE, and OPTIONS scanning methods discussed earlier in this chapter.

```
sipcrack 0.1  ( majomu | www.remote-exploit.org )
------------------------------------------------

* reading and parsing dump file...
* found accounts:

num    server          client          user   algorithm   hash / password
1      192.168.19.81   192.168.19.120  500    plain       12345
2      192.168.19.81   192.168.19.120  500    plain       34after12
3      192.168.19.81   192.168.19.120  500    md5         d3bc10e4f2c9c275fe7da2f20f17600f
4      192.168.19.81   192.168.19.120  500    md5         e5827d8cda285252d5ce87ad8e3c64ca
5      192.168.19.81   192.168.19.120  500    md5         6524e36531b0dd77efa87cede26b4af3

* select which entry to crack (1 - 5): 3

* generating static md5 hash...1a24e68fa4904bd8ce0b7a2b37fffab2
* starting bruteforce against user '500' (md5 hash: 'd3bc10e4f2c9c275fe7da2f20f17600f')
* loaded wordlist: 'big-wordlist.txt'
* tried 8462686 passwords in 13 seconds
* found password: 'a1b2c3'
* updating 'logins-sip.txt'...done
```

Source: http://remote-exploit.org/codes_sipcrack.html. Accessed 2007.

Figure 3-9   SIPcrack sniffs and cracks SIP logins.

SIPcrack

SIPcrack is a SIP login sniffer/cracker that contains two programs: sipdump and sipcrack. The sipdump tool dumps SIP digest authentications. If a login is found, the sniffed login is written to the dump file. The sipcrack tool uses the dump file generated by sipdump to brute-force-attack the user's password. If a password is found, the login is updated in the dump file. SIPcrack is shown in Figure 3-9.

VoIPaudit

VoIPaudit is a VoIP vulnerability assessment and penetration testing tool that assists in the following:

- Identifying network vulnerabilities
- Determining the specific details of security issues and the possible outcomes of leaving them unsecured
- Quickly determining fixes for vulnerabilities

iWar

iWar is a UNIX wardialer. It is written entirely in C, and its features include the following:

- Full logging records all possible events during dialing (busy signals, no answers, carriers, etc.), while default logging only records potentially useful information (carriers, possible telecommunications equipment, etc.)
- ASCII flat file and MySQL logging
- Dials randomly or sequentially
- When finding a remote modem and connecting, iWar will remain connected and attempt to identify the remote system type
- When actively listening to iWar work, anything interesting can be manually marked by pressing a key, and a note can be entered about it
- Multiple modem support
- Full control over the modem
- Blacklisted phone number support
- Saves state to file and can be resumed later
- Loads pregenerated list of numbers
- Records remote system banners on connection for later review
- Can be used to attack PBX and voice mail systems
- Real-time terminal window
- Supports IAX2 VoIP without additional hardware, acting as a full VoIP client with the computer's speakers and microphone, and allowing users to set their own caller ID numbers

VoIP Packet Creation and Flooding Tools

sipsak

The sipsak tool is a small command-line tool for developers and administrators of Session Initiation Protocol (SIP) applications. It can be used for some simple tests on SIP applications and devices. Its features include the following:

- Sends OPTIONS requests
- Sends text files (which should contain SIP requests)
- Traces routes
- Performs user location and flooding tests
- Short notation support for receiving (not for sending)
- Unlimited string replacements in files and requests
- Adds any header to requests
- Simulates calls in usrloc mode
- Uses symmetric signaling to work behind NAT
- Uploads any given contact to a registrar
- Sends messages to any SIP destination

- Searches for strings in reply with regular expressions
- Reads SIP message from stdin
- Supports UDP and TCP transport

SIPp

SIPp is an open-source SIP test tool and traffic generator. It includes a few basic SipStone user agent scenarios (UAC and UAS) and establishes and releases multiple calls with the INVITE and BYE methods. It can also read custom XML scenario files describing call flows. SIPp can be used to test many types of SIP equipment, including SIP proxies, B2BUAs, SIP media servers, SIP/x gateways, and SIP PBX. It is capable of emulating thousands of user agents calling the SIP system.

SIPp is shown in Figure 3-10, and its features include the following:

- Dynamic display of statistics, including call rate, round-trip delay, and message statistics
- Periodic CSV statistics dumps
- Dynamically adjustable call rates
- Supports IPv6, TLS, and SIP authentication
- Conditional scenarios
- UDP retransmissions
- Call-specific variables
- Field injection from an external CSV file to emulate live users

SIPNess Messenger

SIPNess Messenger is a basic tool for learning how SIP sessions are performed, as well as for initial testing and debugging of SIP terminals. It provides the user with an easy way to construct and send proper SIP messages to a remote SIP terminal, and at the same time, receive and monitor incoming SIP messages from remote SIP terminals. SIP messages are formatted and displayed, including their SDP (Session Description Protocol) fields.

SIPNess Messenger supports the following messages:

- INVITE
- RINGING
- TRYING

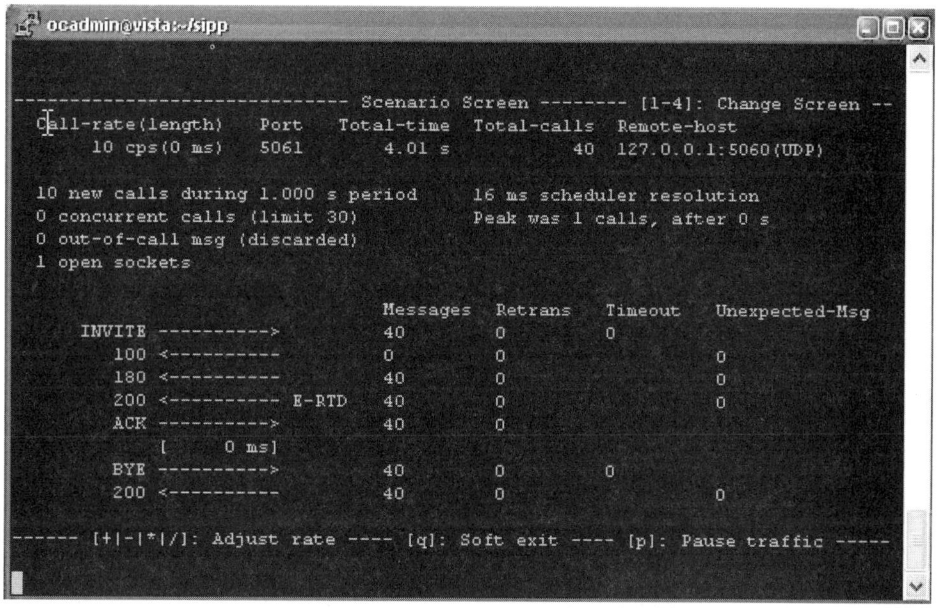

Source: http://sipp.sourceforge.net/. Accessed 2007.

Figure 3-10 SIPp is a SIP test tool and traffic generator.

- CANCEL
- BYE
- ACK
- OK
- REGISTER

The following are the instructions for using SIPNess Messenger:

1. *Sending an INVITE*:
   - Select **INVITE** from the Message Type submenu.
   - Type the username in the **User** field.
   - Type the IP address of the target SIP terminal and the UDP port on which it expects to receive incoming SIP messages.
   - Click the **From** button. A new window will be opened for entering the **VIA** field.
   - Edit the **Subject** field as desired.
   - Press the **Send** button to transmit the message. Please note that the outgoing message will be displayed in the **Message Monitor** window.

2. *Receiving a SIP message*: SIPNess Messenger constantly checks for incoming messages on port 5060. When a message is received, it is displayed in the **Message Monitor** window. The proper fields are copied to the internal database, and these are inserted into subsequent outgoing messages.

3. *Saving a SIP session log file*: The user can save the current content of the **Message Monitor** window to a log file by pressing the **Save** button and specifying the target log file.

4. *Sending a special SIP message*: SIPNess Messenger allows the user to send special SIP messages. SIP messages that were copied from the **Message Monitor** window or from an external file can be pasted into the test SIP window, and modified as desired by the user before being sent by pressing the **OK** button.

SIPNess Messenger is shown in Figure 3-11.

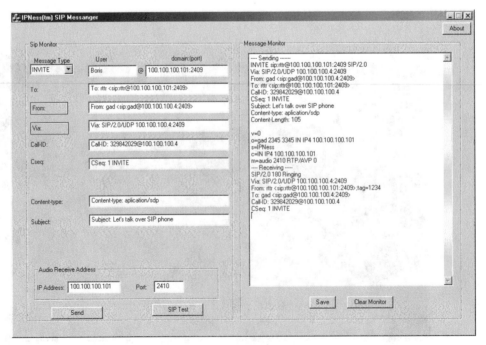

Figure 3-11   SIPNess Messenger is used in the initial testing and debugging of SIP terminals.

SipBomber

SipBomber is a SIP testing tool for Linux. It is shown in Figure 3-12, and its parameters are the following:

- *sip server*: IP or hostname of SIP server
- *udp port*: Server UDP port
- *tcp port*: Server TCP port
- *reparse rand param*: Maximal quantity of not mandate element in BNF rule
- *n-send*: Times the test will be run
- *n-resend*: Times a packet will be resent if nothing is received in response
- *username*: Username of caller
- *username2*: Username of called user
- *password*: Password of username
- *password2*: Password of username2
- *pause*: Pause between REGISTER and INVITE

Spitter

Spitter uses the Asterisk IP PBX platform to launch SPIT calls in order to test, audit, and uncover security vulnerabilities in VoIP infrastructures. Spitter requires read permission to the directory containing the input file, and read/write permission to both the /tmp directory and Asterisk's /var/spool/asterisk/outgoing/ directory.

The input file of SPIT targets contains one or more Asterisk ASCII call records. Spitter processes the records in order, beginning at the top of the file. It creates a file in the /tmp directory for each record. When all call operations related to the call file are completed, Asterisk removes the call file. If the number of files found are greater than or equal to the **limit** option, Spitter stalls and checks the number of files every 10 seconds. When

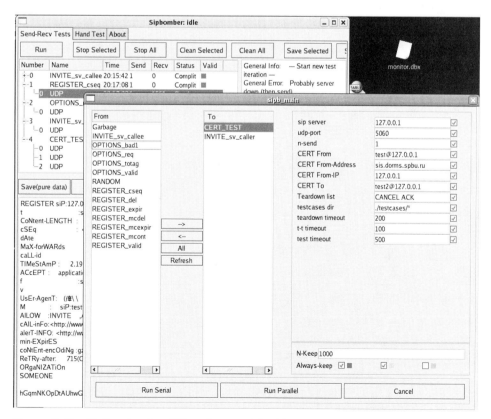

Figure 3-12   SipBomber is a SIP testing tool for Linux.

the number of call files in the outgoing folder drops below the limit, Spitter resumes dropping call files until call records in the input file are exhausted or the outgoing folder is saturated with call files once again.

To Spitter, each call record is simply a series of nonblank lines. Records are separated by a line beginning with the newline character. Spitter creates a separate file for each record, but does not parse the lines in a record to confirm its completeness.

Sip Send Fun

Sip Send Fun is a tiny command-line script that exploits vulnerabilities using Netcat to send different SIP payloads to the target device. It includes the following functions:

- Payload
  - New-Message
  - No-New-Message
  - INVITE
- Test of a single device or a class-C scan
- Source-IP spoofing
- Send payload to a single port or perform a port scan

Other VoIP Tools

VoIP Fuzzing Tools

- Asteroid
- Codenomicon VoIP Fuzzers
- Fuzzy Packet
- Interstate Fuzzer
- ohrwurm
- PROTOS H.323 Fuzzer
- PROTOS SIP Fuzzer
- SIP Forum Test Framework (SFTF)
- SIP Proxy

VoIP Signaling Manipulation Tools

- BYE Teardown
- Check Sync Phone Rebooter
- H225regregject
- IAXAuthJack
- IAXHangup
- RedirectPoison
- Registration Adder
- Registration Eraser
- Registration Hijacker
- SIP-Kill
- SIP-Proxy-Kill
- SIP-RedirectRTP
- SipRogue
- VoIP Network Attack Toolkit
- VoIPHopper

VoIP Media Manipulation Tools

- RTP InsertSound
- RTP MixSound
- RTPInject
- RTPProxy
- SteganRTP
- Vo²IP

Chapter Summary

- VoIP security threats can be divided into the following three categories: attacks against the VoIP devices, configuration faults in VoIP devices, and IP infrastructure attacks.

- The following are various VoIP attacks: reconnaissance attacks, protocol fuzzing, denial-of-service (DoS) attacks, call hijacking and redirection, VoIP spam, spoofing, eavesdropping, and session anomalies.

- Many VoIP phones use a Trivial File Transfer Protocol (TFTP) server to download configuration settings each time they power on.

- VoIPong detects all Voice over IP calls on a pipeline.

- Sip Send Fun is a tiny command-line-based script that exploits vulnerabilities.

- Spitter is a tool that uses the Asterisk IP PBX as a platform from which to launch SPIT calls.

- Netdude is a front end to the libnetdude packet manipulation library.

## Chapter 4

VPN Penetration Testing

Objectives

After completing this chapter, you should be able to:

- Test virtual private networks (VPNs)
- Use tools for testing virtual private networks (VPNs)

Key Terms

Backoff strategy the way a server deals with lost packets

Introduction to VPN Penetration Testing

A virtual private network (VPN) uses the Internet to provide secure access to remote offices or users within the same enterprise network. Figure 4-1 is a diagram of a VPN.

VPN penetration testing ensures that the VPN is sufficiently private and secure. This chapter teaches you how to perform the testing on both types of VPNs (IPSec and SSL).

VPN Penetration Testing Steps

Step 1: Scanning

Testers should first check the state of common VPN ports such as 500 (UDP IPSec), 1723 (TCP PPTP), and 443 (TCP/SSL).

Scan 500 (UDP IPSec)

Figure 4-2 shows Nmap discovering the ISAKMP service, which is the IPSec VPN server, looking for UDP port 500.

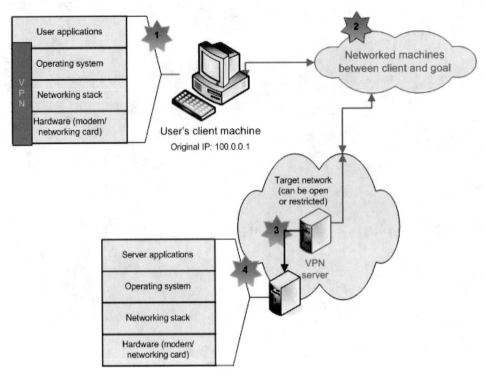

Figure 4-1 This diagram shows the basic layout of a VPN.

```
owner:~# nmap -P0 -sU -p 500 192.168.0.1


Starting nmap 3.55 ( http://www.insecure.org/nmap/ ) at 2004-08-14 09:51 ART
Interesting ports on target.com (192.168.0.1):
PORT   STATE SERVICE
500/udp open  isakmp


Nmap run completed -- 1 IP address (1 host up) scanned in 12.671 seconds
```

Figure 4-2 This is an example of Nmap discovering the ISAKMP service, looking for an open UDP port 500.

Scan 1723 (TCP PPTP)

PPTP uses TCP port 1723 to establish a connection with a remote VPN server. Figure 4-3 shows Nmap discovering PPTP.

The dsniff tool can be used to identify some security flaws in PPTP, as shown in the following example:

```
dsniff
dsniff: listening on eth0
08/15/04 03:05:13 gre 192.168.0.1 -> vpnserver.com (pptp)
DOMAIN\Username:0:9B310870A8D1CXEC:00000000000000000000000000000000000000000
00000000:6AF13DCD112407WDCSS04E398851DD4F40BEDECCCF3D6FE13D
```

```
owner:~# nmap -P0 -sT -p 1723 192.168.0.1


Starting nmap 3.55 ( http://www.insecure.org/nmap/ ) at 2004-08-14 09:55 ART
Interesting ports on target.com (192.168.0.1):
PORT     STATE SERVICE
1723/tcp open  pptp


Nmap run completed -- 1 IP address (1 host up) scanned in 0.962 seconds
```

Figure 4-3   This shows Nmap finding a PPTP VPN server on TCP port 1723.

Scan 443 (TCP/SSL)

SSL-based VPNs use standard Web-based protocols on TCP port 443, so testers should check that port.

Scan with nmap -sU -P0 -p 500

This Nmap command uses the following options:

- **-sU:** UDP scan
- **-P0:** Treat all hosts as online, skipping host discovery
- **-p 500:** Only scan port 500

Thus, the following command will perform a UDP scan for port 500 on all hosts from 192.168.0.1 through 192.168.0.255:

```
nmap -sU -P0 -p 500 192.168.0.1-255
```

Scan with IPSecScan

Similar to Nmap, IPSecScan can scan either a single IP address or a range of IP addresses to search for systems using IPSec. The following shows example IPSecScan output:

```
ipsecscan.exe 192.168.0.1 192.168.0.2

IPSecScan 1.1 - (c) 2001, Arne Vidstrom, arne.vidstrom@ntsecurity.nu

- http://ntsecurity.nu/toolbox/ipsecscan/

192.168.0.1 IPSec status: Enabled

192.168.0.2 IPSec status: Indeterminable
```

Step 2: Fingerprinting

The fingerprinting process provides the following information about a VPN server:

- Vendor
- Model
- Software version

There are various fingerprinting techniques that can be used to identify these details, which can greatly assist an attacker in assessing a VPN's vulnerabilities and its default usernames and passwords.

Internet Key Exchange (IKE) is part of IPSec. The IKE-Scan tool uses its own retransmission strategy to deal with lost packets in order to fingerprint a VPN server. The tool sends an IKE packet to probe the VPN server, but it does not reply to the VPN server's responses. This makes the server believe that the packets are lost, so

```
G:\ike-VPN-test>ike-scan 10.0.0.1
Starting ike-scan 1.6 with 1 hosts (http://www.nta-monitor.com/ike-scan/)
10.0.0.1 Main Mode Handshake returned SA=(Enc=3DES Hash=SHA1 Auth=PSK Group=1:modp768 LifeT
ype=Seconds LifeDuration(4)=0x00007080)

Ending ike-scan 1.6: 1 hosts scanned in 0.979 seconds (1.02 hosts/sec).
1 returned handshake; 0 returned notify
```

Figure 4-4   Try all combinations of transform attributes until one is returned.

```
$ ike-scan -M --trans=5,2,1,2 --showbackoff 10.0.0.1
Starting ike-scan 1.7 with 1 hosts (http://www.nta-monitor.com/ike-scan/)
10.0.0.1       Main Mode Handshake returned
        SA=(Enc=3DES Hash=SHA1 Auth=PSK Group=2:modp1024 LifeType=Seconds LifeDuration(4)=0x00007080

IKE Backoff Patterns:

IP Address     No.     Recv time               Delta Time
10.0.0.1       1       1121251508.773117       0.000000
10.0.0.1       2       1121251510.772474       1.999357
10.0.0.1       3       1121251512.775259       2.002785
10.0.0.1       4       1121251514.777952       2.002693
10.0.0.1       5       1121251516.780746       2.002794
10.0.0.1       6       1121251518.783504       2.002758
10.0.0.1       7       1121251520.786298       2.002794
10.0.0.1       8       1121251524.791781       4.005483
10.0.0.1       9       1121251528.797329       4.005548
10.0.0.1       10      1121251532.802822       4.005493
10.0.0.1       11      1121251536.808370       4.005548
10.0.0.1       12      1121251540.813874       4.005504
10.0.0.1       Implementation guess: Firewall-1 4.1/NG/NGX
```

Figure 4-5   UDP backoff fingerprinting takes between one and two minutes.

the server tries to resend the lost packets according to its *backoff strategy*. The way the server tries to resend these packets, including the time difference between the packets and the amount of retries before it gives up, can allow IKE-Scan to fingerprint the server.

Get the IKE Handshake

The first step of fingerprinting is to get the IKE handshake from each system that is to be fingerprinted. Testers note the suitable transform attributes from the Security Association (SA) payload. Then, they try all combinations of transform attributes until one is returned, as shown in Figure 4-4.

Perform UDP Backoff Fingerprinting

The -showbackoff option of IKE-Scan records the response time of all packets, and it delays for 60 seconds after the last packet is received. This delay ensures that all packets are received before displaying the results. Using this option, backoff fingerprinting usually takes between one and two minutes.

Figure 4-5 shows an example of UDP backoff fingerprinting using IKE-Scan. The results are divided into the following columns:

- *IP Address*: The IP address of the target VPN server.
- *No.*: The number of the response packet from this host; the first response packet starts at 1.
- *Recv time*: The time when the response packet was received, measured in epoch time.
- *Delta Time*: This column shows the difference in time between when the scan began and when a particular packet was received.

Perform Vendor ID Fingerprinting

The vendor ID payload contains both arbitrary and payload data. The payload is always an MD5 hash of a text string. Vendors use these payloads for various purposes, such as exchanging proprietary details and recognizing their own system implementation.

```
$ ike-scan --trans=5,2,3,2 --multiline 10.0.0.4
Starting ike-scan 1.7 with 1 hosts (http://www.nta-monitor.com/ike-scan/)
10.0.0.4 Main Mode Handshake returned
        SA=(Enc=3DES Hash=SHA1 Group=2:modp1024 Auth=RSA_Sig LifeType=Seconds LifeDuration(4)=0x0000
        VID=1e2b516905991c7d7c96fcbfb587e46100000004 (Windows-2003-or-XP-SP2)
        VID=4048b7d56ebce88525e7de7f00d6c2d3 (IKE Fragmentation)
        VID=90cb80913ebb696e086381b5ec427b1f (draft-ietf-ipsec-nat-t-ike-02\n)
```

```
$ ike-scan --trans=5,2,1,2 --vendor=f4ed19e0c114eb516faaac0ee37daf2807b4381f --multiline 10.0.0.1
Starting ike-scan 1.7 with 1 hosts (http://www.nta-monitor.com/ike-scan/)
10.0.0.1    Main Mode Handshake returned
        SA=(Enc=3DES Hash=SHA1 Auth=PSK Group=2:modp1024 LifeType=Seconds LifeDuration(4)=0x00007080
        VID=f4ed19e0c114eb516faaac0ee37daf2807b4381f000000010000138c000000000000000018a00000 (Firewa
```

```
$ ike-scan --trans=5,2,1,2 --vendor=00 --multiline 10.0.0.3
Starting ike-scan 1.7 with 1 hosts (http://www.nta-monitor.com/ike-scan/)
10.0.0.3    Main Mode Handshake returned
        SA=(Enc=3DES Hash=SHA1 Auth=PSK Group=2:modp1024 LifeType=Seconds LifeDuration(4)=0x00007080
        VID=424e455300000009 (Nortel Contivity)
```

Figure 4-6   IKE-Scan automatically displays vendor ID payloads.

```
$ ike-scan --aggressive --multiline --id=finance_group 10.0.0.2
Starting ike-scan 1.7 with 1 hosts (http://www.nta-monitor.com/ike-scan/)
10.0.0.2 Aggressive Mode Handshake returned
        SA=(Enc=3DES Hash=MD5 Group=2:modp1024 Auth=PSK LifeType=Seconds LifeDuration=28800)
        KeyExchange(128 bytes)
        Nonce(20 bytes)
        ID(Type=ID_IPV4_ADDR, Value=10.0.0.2)
        Hash(16 bytes)
        VID=12f5f28c457168a9702d9fe274cc0100 (Cisco Unity)
        VID=09002689dfd6b712 (XAUTH)
        VID=afcad71368a1f1c96b8696fc77570100 (Dead Peer Detection)
        VID=4048b7d56ebce88525e7de7f00d6c2d3c0000000 (IKE Fragmentation)
        VID=1f07f70eaa6514d3b0fa96542a500306 (Cisco VPN Concentrator)
```

```
$ ike-scan --trans=7/256,2,1,2 --aggressive --multiline 192.168.91.2
Starting ike-scan 1.7 with 1 hosts (http://www.nta-monitor.com/ike-scan/)
192.168.91.2        Aggressive Mode Handshake returned
        SA=(Enc=AES KeyLength=256 Hash=SHA1 Group=2:modp1024 Auth=PSK LifeType=Seconds LifeDuration=
        VID=09002689dfd6b712 (XAUTH)
        VID=afcad71368a1f1c96b8696fc77570100 (Dead Peer Detection)
        VID=12f5f28c457168a9702d9fe274cc0100 (Cisco Unity)
        VID=11f27f551d0760dfc9ca6f5670fe5291
        KeyExchange(128 bytes)
        ID(Type=ID_FQDN, Value=pix520-internet.company.com)
        Nonce(20 bytes)
        Hash(20 bytes)
```

Figure 4-7   It can be difficult to handshake with servers using aggressive mode.

IKE-Scan automatically displays vendor ID payloads, as shown in Figure 4-6. Testers can add the payload packet into an outgoing packet by using the **-vendor** option.

Check for IKE Aggressive Mode

Testers can use the aggressive mode of the IKE-Scan tool to determine if the server supports aggressive mode. If it does, it can be difficult to handshake with the server, because it will not respond until a valid ID is supplied in the identification payload. Figure 4-7 shows IKE-Scan in aggressive mode.

Step 3: PSK Crack

Testers can use IKE-Scan with the -pskcrack option to obtain IKE aggressive mode preshared keys through brute force or dictionary attacks. Then, testers can use IKEProbe to identify the vulnerabilities in the PSK implementation of the VPN server. By attempting various combinations of ciphers, hashes, and Diffie-Hellman groups, IKEProbe forces the VPN server into aggressive mode. The following is an example of IKEProbe output:

```
IKEProbe 0.1beta (c) 2003 Michael Thumann (www.ernw.de)

Portions Copyright (c) 2003 Cipherica Labs
```

```
(www.cipherica.com)

Read license-cipherica.txt for LibIKE License Information

IKE Aggressive Mode PSK Vulnerability Scanner (Bugtraq ID
7423)

Supported Attributes

Ciphers : DES, 3DES, AES-128, CAST

Hashes : MD5, SHA1

Diffie Hellman Groups: DH Groups 1,2 and 5

IKE Proposal for Peer: 10.0.0.2

Aggressive Mode activated . . .

[Output truncated for brevity]

Cipher AES

Hash MD5

Diffie Hellman Group 2

841.890 3: ph1 _ initiated(00443ee0, 007d23c8)

841.950 3: << ph1 (00443ee0, 276)

843.963 3: << ph1 (00443ee0, 276)

846.967 3: << ph1 (00443ee0, 276)

849.961 3: ph1 _ disposed(00443ee0)

Attribute Settings:

Cipher AES

Hash MD5

Diffie Hellman Group 5

849.961 3: ph1 _ initiated(00443ee0, 007d5010)

849.141 3: << ph1 (00443ee0, 340)

851.644 3: << ph1 (00443ee0, 340)

854.648 3: << ph1 (00443ee0, 340)

857.652 3: ph1 _ disposed(00443ee0)

[Output has been truncated]
```

Next, either the Cain & Abel tool or IKECrack can be used to crack the sniffed preshared key. Once this key has been obtained, it can be used with the PGPNet tool to connect to the VPN server.

Step 4: Test for Default User Accounts

Like other network devices and services, VPN software has default user accounts at the time of installation. Although administrators would be wise to change these accounts immediately, many do not, allowing attackers to use these default accounts to login. Using the information obtained in the fingerprinting stage, a simple Web search can reveal the default user accounts and passwords.

Check for Unencrypted Usernames in a File or the Registry

A username is often stored in an unencrypted file or the Windows registry, making it easily accessible to anyone with access to the user's computer. Figure 4-8 shows a username stored in plaintext in the registry. Once that username is obtained, testers can use IKE-Scan in aggressive mode to find the password.

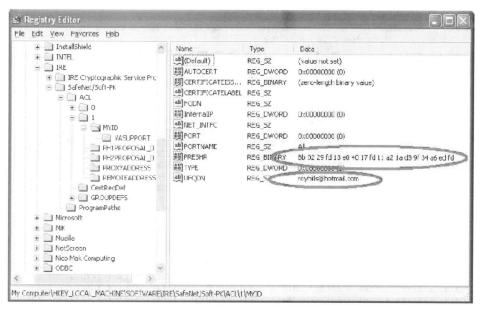

Figure 4-8   Sometimes, usernames are stored in plaintext in the registry.

Test for Plaintext Password

VPN client applications store plaintext passwords in memory. Any person who has access to the client's computer can easily get the password from the VPN system. Once a VPN client has been found, testers can use dumping tools such as PMDump to obtain the password. After completing the dumping process, testers can crash the computer to get a complete dump of physical memory.

Figure 4-9 shows the plaintext password in memory.

Step 5: Test SSL VPN

Scanning a Web-based SSL VPN is similar to scanning an IPSec VPN. Testers can use the following tools:

- IKE-Scan
- IPSecScan
- IKEProbe
- PGPnet

In addition, testers should check if the SSL VPN is vulnerable to standard Web-based threats, such as the following:

- Cross-site scripting
- SQL injection
- Weak authentication
- Buffer overflow

Tools such as WebInspect and Watchfire check for these threats.

Tools for VPN Penetration Testing

IKE-Scan

IKE-Scan is a command-line tool that uses the IKE protocol to discover, fingerprint, and test IPSec VPN servers. It supports preshared key cracking in IKE aggressive mode using preshared key authentication. Figure 4-10 shows IKE-Scan.

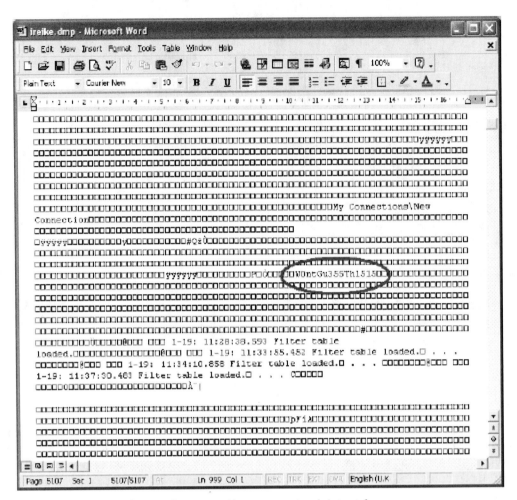

Figure 4-9 Passwords are often stored in memory in plaintext form.

IKEProbe

IKEProbe can be used to determine the vulnerabilities in the preshared key implementation of VPN servers. By using different combinations of ciphers, hashes, and Diffie-Hellman groups, it attempts to force the server into aggressive mode.

VPNmonitor

VPNmonitor is a free Java tool for observing network traffic. It can monitor the VPN (PPTP and IPSec) and SSL (HTTPS) connectivity of both wired and wireless networks. It displays a graphical representation of network traffic, as shown in Figure 4-11.

IKECrack

IKECrack analyzes and cracks preshared keys that use RFC-compliant aggressive mode authentication. It uses brute force and dictionary attacks on the keys.

PGPnet

PGPnet is a complete IPSec implementation. It allows secure connections to any other PGPnet/IPSec host on the Internet regardless of whether the user has communicated with that host previously, without preconfiguration of that host.

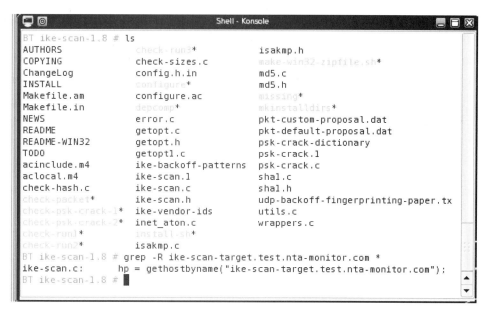

Figure 4-10   IKE-Scan discovers, fingerprints, and tests IPSec VPN servers.

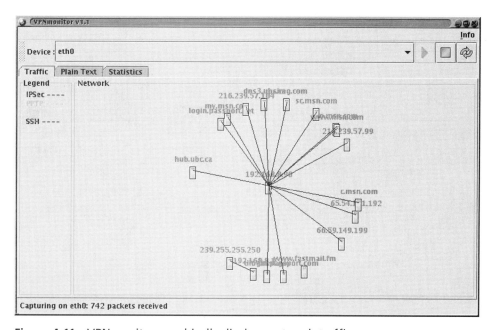

Figure 4-11   VPNmonitor graphically displays network traffic.

Chapter Summary

- A virtual private network (VPN) uses the Internet to provide secure access to remote offices or users within the same enterprise network.

- There are two types of VPNs: IPSec and SSL.

- The first step in a VPN penetration test is to check the state of common VPN ports such as 500 (UDP IPSec), 1723 (TCP PPTP), and 443 (TCP/SSL).

- The fingerprinting process provides the following information about a VPN server: vendor, model, and software version.
- The first step of fingerprinting is to get the IKE handshake from each system that is to be fingerprinted.
- Testers can use the aggressive mode of the IKE-Scan tool to see if the server supports aggressive mode.
- A username is often stored in an unencrypted file or the Windows registry, making it easily accessible to anyone with access to the user's computer.

## Chapter 5

Wardialing

Objectives

After completing this chapter, you should be able to:

- Understand the concept of wardialing
- Perform wardialing penetration testing
- Select the proper software for wardialing penetration testing
- Describe some of the tools used for wardialing
- Describe the Sandtrap tool, a countermeasure for wardialing

Key Terms

Wardialing the exploitation of an organization's telephone, modem, and private branch exchange (PBX) system to infiltrate the internal network in order to abuse computing resources

Introduction to Wardialing

Today, dial-up modems are no longer the most common way to access external network resources, such as the Internet. However, organizations still use modems for remote access solutions, and some organizations may have legacy dial-up modems that they do not even know about. These modems can allow a savvy attacker to gain unauthorized access to a system. This chapter teaches you about wardialing and how to perform a wardialing penetration test. It also covers some of the tools used in this type of penetration test.

Wardialing Overview

Wardialing is the exploitation of an organization's telephone, modem, and private branch exchange (PBX) system to infiltrate the internal network in order to abuse computing resources. Most PBX systems are being manufactured with increased security configurations; however, there are still many insecure modems that can be compromised to gain access to target systems.

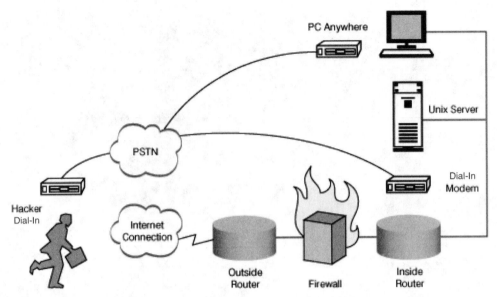

Figure 5-1   An attacker can bypass firewalls and other security features by using wardialing to dial in to an organization's modems.

What had initially caught the fancy of hackers in the movie *WarGames* still manages to find vulnerable modems, leading to compromise of systems. The wardialer program in *WarGames* was not highly developed, as it only found phone numbers that it assumed to be computer dial-in lines. A hostile version of a wardialer generally tries to find out the operating system and much more, for example, usernames and active services.

The relevance of wardialers today arises from the fact that though Internet connections have firewalls and intrusion detection systems installed, modems are still often unsecured. In some cases, they are left connected to the network and simply forgotten about. Wardialers differ from daemon dialers, in that the former targets a large collection of telephone numbers, while the latter targets a single phone number. As remote users are increasing, so are remote dial-in connections to networks. Some of these remote users may not be using security precautions, such as personal firewalls, thereby allowing intruders to access the main network.

Figure 5-1 shows how an attacker can bypass an organization's security measures using wardialing.

Wardialing Techniques

There are various techniques for performing wardialing. The first process is to compile every public telephone number in the company. This determines how many and what types of equipment are used in the organization.

Dial inventory classification is another wardialing technique. This process is used to classify usable telephone resources. After classifying the dial inventory, an attacker can use various tools to find out exactly which devices are active.

Many organizations and security professionals use wardialing programs and wardialing classification techniques to assess the security posture of an organization. The following are three wardialing techniques:

1. *Basic wardialing sweep (BWS)*: In this technique, the wardialing software calls a range of phone numbers without human intervention and identifies a set of known carrier signals.

2. *Multiple wardialing sweep (MWS)*: In this technique, a basic wardialing sweep (BWS) is conducted sequentially by using a range of configuration parameters and conditions. It conducts a separate sweep for each device type, such as a fax machine.

3. *Attended wardialing sweep (AWS)*: In this technique, the software dials a range of phone numbers while a professional listener is in attendance to detect irregular behavior and unknown devices.

Most security professionals prefer AWS to BWS and MWS. BWS and MWS have various drawbacks, including the following:

- Inability to detect voice mail
- Inability to detect ISDN equipment
- More false negatives
- Conflicting results
- Higher cost

Reasons to Conduct Wardialing Penetration Tests

Wardialing penetration testing is conducted to check whether:

- Anyone from an organization has attached a modem to the network
- An organization's authorized modems are vulnerable to wardialers
- Modems reveal banners and their identity
- Devices such as fax machines on an organization's PBX are accessible from the PSTN (public switched telephone network)
- Any of an organization's modems use default passwords
- There is unknown open access to an organization's systems
- Security audits across an organization are regularly conducted or not
- An organization's network contains security holes

Prerequisites for Wardialing Penetration Testing

Wardialing penetration testing is used to protect and secure an organization's network infrastructure. There are various authorizations and policy-related rules that need to be recognized before conducting a wardialing penetration testing. The following are some of the basic prerequisites for conducting such a penetration test:

- *Confirmation about the range of numbers to be dialed*: The penetration tester must inform the organization about the range of numbers that are going to be dialed.
- *Approval from the organization*: The penetration tester must first receive permission to conduct a wardialing test on the system to avoid legal issues.
- *Authorization from the telephone company*: The tester should check the local telephone company rules and obtain permission from telephone service providers if necessary.
- *Notification to all parties that may be affected*: The tester should explain the modalities of wardialing to all parties that may be affected, to avoid any negative consequences.
- *Agreement for date and time*: The tester must confirm the date and time of the wardialing attempt with the organization.
- *Exclusion of business-critical systems*: The penetration tester must clarify all exclusions beforehand. Organizations may prohibit wardialing attempts on certain business-critical systems.

Some organizations have policies that do not allow the use of modems without proper authentication, but the majority do not have such policies.

Software Selection for Wardialing

A wardialer is a program that sequentially dials a range of phone numbers and negotiates a connection if possible. A wardialer software program is the main tool for wardialing. THC-Scan and ToneLoc are the best-known examples of wardialing tools.

There are three common categories of wardialers:

1. *Commercial wardialing software*: This software is used for specific modem pools or remote access solutions.

2. *Homegrown wardialing software*: Network administrators develop this type of software for use by network operation centers to find out if they can get a phone number to pick up an incoming call.

3. *Hackerware wardialing software*: Hackers generally use this type of software. Attackers may conceal callback schemes into this software, which can monitor and record data flows. The software may then stealthily send e-mail that contains private information. When selecting hackerware, testers should take the proper precautions.

Guidelines for Configuring Wardialing Software

The most important criterion for conducting a proper wardialing penetration test is to use properly configured wardialing software. Many standard, slow-phase protocol devices require numerous synchronized settings. Higher-end modems require a voice and data setting to identify telephone resources.

The following are some guidelines for configuring different wardialing software:

- Check the country option, because different countries have different dial tones, which may confuse the modem. Adjust the dial tone according to the particular country.

- If possible, turn on error control. Use MNP (Microcom Network Protocol) for error control.

- Select the proper detection level to detect voice, fax, carriers, tones, and voice mail.

- Check the fax recognition. Fax devices use various protocols to negotiate a connection. Keep fax modems in fax mode or data mode.

- Try to use hardware flow control.

- Check the modem command set and ensure that the modem accepts standard Hayes and AT commands.

- Check whether the organization's PBX or switch supports the necessary dialing features.

- Keep the serial port at the proper speed. Most ports can support 115,200 baud, but by default they are set to 9,600 baud. Adjust the port speed according to your requirements.

- Check the timeout option and allocate enough time per phone.

- Check the phone service and ensure that it supports voice mail, call forwarding, and call waiting.

- If possible, turn off data compression.

Recommendations for Establishing an Effective Wardialing Penetration Testing Process

The wardialing process is simple, and wardialing can be dangerous to large organizations. With the increase in remote access points, every modem may be vulnerable.

The following are some recommendations for establishing a useful wardialing penetration testing process:

- Prepare a schedule for regular and routine wardialing penetration testing.

- Prepare a remote access policy for employees.

- Impart training to employees to recognize social engineering techniques.

Generally, wardialing attacks go unnoticed, so organizations should identify any vulnerabilities to protect themselves against attacks.

Interpreting Wardialing Penetration Testing Results

Results of wardialing penetration testing may include a large number of active modems and PBX systems. These results should be systematically collected in a database so that they can be easily correlated and interpreted. Results should be sorted based on different parameters to allow the testing team to analyze the results. If the penetration test detects any unauthorized devices, then the tester should remove or shut off that device.

Wardialing Tools

The following are some tools used for wardialing:

- A-Dial
- Assault Dialer
- Autoscan
- BASTap
- Bbeep
- BlueDial
- Carrier
- Catcall
- Code Thief Deluxe
- CyberPhreak
- Deluxe Fone-Code Hacker
- Demon Dialer
- Dialer
- Dialing Demon
- Doo Tools
- DTMF_d
- Fear's Phreaker Tools
- GunBelt
- HyperTerminal
- Laplink
- Mhunter
- ModemScan
- OkiPad
- PBX Scanner
- pcAnywhere
- PhoneSweep
- PhoneTag
- PhreakMaster
- Procomm Plus
- Professor Falken's Phreak Tools
- Scavenger Dialer
- SecureLogix
- Super Dial
- THC-Scan
- The Little Operator
- ToneLoc
- Ultra-Dial
- VrACK
- WildDialer
- X-Dialer
- Zhacker

PhoneSweep

Sandstorm's PhoneSweep (Figure 5-2) is a popular commercial wardialer. The following are some of the benefits of PhoneSweep:

- PhoneSweep is easy to use, flexible, and powerful.
- It dials every number in an organization.
- It is a robust multiline scanner, which scales to meet the user's specific requirements.
- Once the installation is complete, PhoneSweep will:
  - Identify computers running remote access software to bypass the corporate firewall.

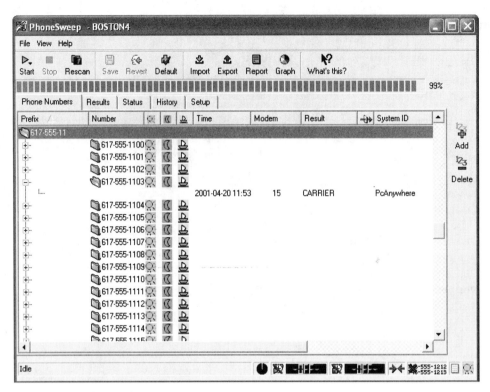

Figure 5-2 PhoneSweep dials a range of numbers and reports those that are accepting connections or are running remote access software.

- Identify over 460 systems and try to break in.
- Identify approved or unapproved modems that accept incoming calls.
- Identify critical backup modems that have failed.
- PhoneSweep operates in one of these user-selectable modes:
  - *Connect*: Quickly scans all numbers using patented Single Call Detect technology.
  - *Identify*: Refines scans and identifies numbers that yield a modem connection.
  - *Penetrate*: This is the most aggressive setting, using brute-force passwords against the identified modems.
- It contains versatile username and password-checking functionality.
- It provides stops, starts, and system recovery mid-scan features.
- It produces several customizable reports.

THC-Scan

THC-Scan (Figure 5-3) is a free wardialer released by van Hauser of The Hacker's Choice (THC), a European hacker/phreaker group. THC-Scan was coded as a set of MSDOS-based programs that are designed to be run from the command line with as much automation as possible. What sets THC-Scan apart from other commercial dialers is the flexibility of its internal configuration that decides what to scan for and how to interpret the results. It does not serve the purpose of phone scanning alone and will show any number that behaves unusually, if properly configured.

An attacker can use THC-Scan with THC-LoginHacker to brute-force systems that have been discovered. Because it is an open-source product, hackers can often modify it, as they are able to glean the workings of the application. This wardialer can dial telephone numbers in either a predetermined range or from a given list. The

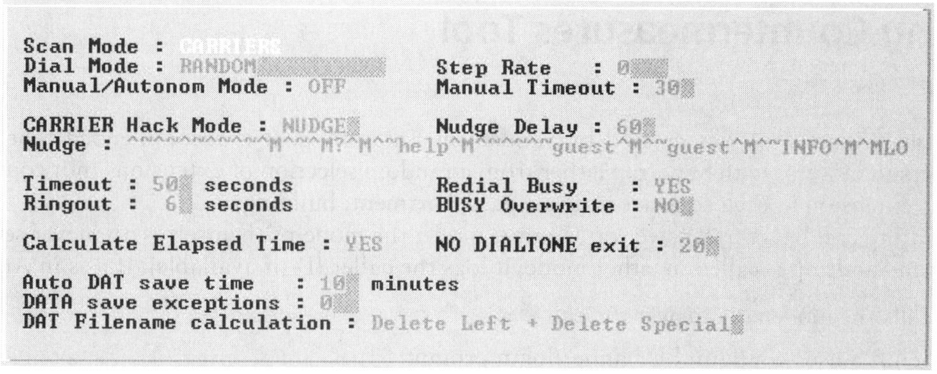

Figure 5-3 THC-Scan is a free wardialer.

scanner also possesses simple identification techniques that can be used to detect answering computer systems or voice-mail boxes (VMBs). A manual mode is also available for users to dial the modem with the speaker enabled. THC-Scan will automatically redial busy numbers up to a preset limit.

Interestingly, THC has features that are designed to facilitate covert use, such as a "boss key" that replaces the computer's screen with an incongruous bitmap and ceases all dialing operations. It automatically determines the parity of the dial-up systems by analyzing the response received from a remote host for a connection request. This is especially useful to an attacker who wants to call back a discovered system and attempt further penetration.

ToneLoc

ToneLoc is one of the most popular wardialing computer programs for MS-DOS. It simply dials numbers, looking for some kind of tone. It is used to do the following:

- Find PBXs
- Find loops or milliwatt test numbers
- Find dial-up long distance carriers
- Find any number that gives a constant tone, or something that a modem will recognize as one
- Find carriers (other modems)
- Hack PBXs

ModemScan

ModemScan is a GUI wardialer software program that utilizes Microsoft Windows Telephony. The following are some of the features of ModemScan:

- Works with hardware the organization already owns and does not require the additional purchase of specific or specialized hardware
- Randomly selects and dials phone numbers from the dial range list to prevent line termination from phone companies that detect sequential dialing
- Runs multiple ModemScan copies with more than one phone line and modem on the same computer
- Imports comma-delimited text files containing phone numbers or ranges of numbers
- Utilizes Microsoft's telephony settings for easy modem and location setup
- Produces reports that may be printed or exported
- Schedules automatic dialing during "off-business" hours
- Saves dialed results using Microsoft's Access database, ensuring database integrity and reliability, while allowing for complex querying and ad hoc reporting
- Watches remote modem's responses from built-in terminal emulation window
- Logs all session events

Wardialing Countermeasures Tool

Sandtrap

Sandtrap (Figure 5-4) was created by Sandstorm Enterprises. It is recommended that the user select phone numbers to monitor with Sandtrap either from a random selection of extensions (not consecutive numbers) or a sample extension in each sensitive range (e.g., department, building).

Sandtrap can be set to Answer or Monitor mode; the modems themselves are never set to Auto-Answer. When Sandtrap is called in either mode, it logs the caller ID (if available). If it is in Answer mode, then it:

- Tells the modem to answer the call
- Sends a user-configurable banner/login prompt
- Sends a user-configurable password prompt if the caller responds
- Sends a user-configurable success or failure message if the caller responds to the password prompt

Finally, Sandtrap logs the information collected and sends a notification, if so configured.

In Answer mode, the caller is kept online in a simulated environment. All text received from the caller is logged to a file and displayed on the user interface. Sandtrap can also notify the user immediately upon being called or upon being connected to, via an e-mail message to an address the user specifies or via HTTP POST to a Web URL the user specifies. Conditions that can be configured to generate notification messages include:

- Incoming caller ID (enabled by default)
- Login attempt (enabled by default)
- Modem disabled due to COM port errors (enabled by default)
- Sandtrap application shutdown

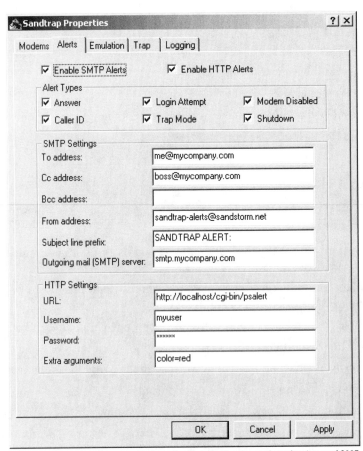

Source: http://www.sandstorm.net/products/sandtrap/screenshots.php. Accessed 2007.

Figure 5-4   Sandtrap allows a user to specify which types of events trigger alerts and how to send those alerts.

Information about system status is displayed by the application's GUI, and optionally on the Windows system tray. The user can tell at a glance the status of a modem: disabled, enabled, listening enabled, ringing enabled, and call in progress.

Sandtrap is distributed with a simple low-overhead Web server, which allows users to create their own CGI-BIN programs to process HTTP notification messages without the security and shared resource issues that might arise from adding this function to an existing server. The distribution contains an example CGI script (psalert.cgi) to work from.

Chapter Summary

- Wardialing involves the use of a program in conjunction with a modem to penetrate the modem-based systems of an organization by continually dialing in.

- Three different types of wardialing techniques are basic wardialing sweep (BWS), multiple wardialing Sweep (MWS), and attended wardialing sweep (AWS).

- In MWS, a BWS is conducted sequentially using a range of configuration parameters and conditions. It conducts a separate sweep for each device type, such as a fax machine.

- In AWS, a range of phone numbers is dialed with a professional listener in attendance to detect irregular behavior and unknown devices.

- The three software categories to perform wardialing are commercial, homegrown, and hackerware.

- If wardialing penetration testing detects any unauthorized devices, then those devices should be removed or shut off.

- THC-Scan is a type of wardialer that scans a defined range of phone numbers.

## Chapter 6

Bluetooth and Handheld Device Penetration Testing

Objectives

After completing this chapter, you should be able to:

- Test the iPhone and iPod touch
- Test the BlackBerry
- Test PDAs
- Test Bluetooth devices

Key Terms

Pairing   the process of associating Bluetooth devices with one another so they can communicate

Piconet   a short-range ad hoc network between Bluetooth devices

Introduction to Bluetooth and Handheld Device Penetration Testing

Today's handheld devices have as much computing power as full desktop computers had just a few years ago. Many people carry a huge amount of personal information in their pockets, and these devices, such as the iPhone, BlackBerry, and Android smartphones, all communicate wirelessly. This means that they are vulnerable to wireless attacks, so they must be tested. This chapter teaches you how to test these devices for common vulnerabilities.

iPhone and iPod touch Penetration Testing

The iPod touch is essentially an iPhone without cellular telephone capabilities. Penetration testing for an iPod touch is very much the same as for the iPhone, except without telephone-specific steps.

Step 1: Jailbreaking

By default, the iPhone and iPod touch will only run software approved by Apple. Jailbreaking is the process of unlocking the iPhone or iPod touch in order to install unlicensed applications, add new ringtones, or change the device's wallpaper. This also makes the file system readable by a computer.

Once an iPhone or iPod touch has been jailbroken, attackers can install malicious software or extract sensitive data. Tools used for jailbreaking include the following:

- iFuntastic
- AppSnapp
- iDemocracy
- iActivator
- iNdependence

iFuntastic

After downloading and installing iFuntastic (Figure 6-1) on a Macintosh computer, the penetration tester should follow these steps:

1. Reboot the system.
2. Switch on the iPhone and connect it to the Macintosh.
3. If iTunes launches automatically, close it.
4. Launch iFuntastic.
5. Click the **Prepare** button on the left side of the iFuntastic window.
6. Click the **Jailbreak** button at the bottom of the window.
7. Follow the six steps in the next window.

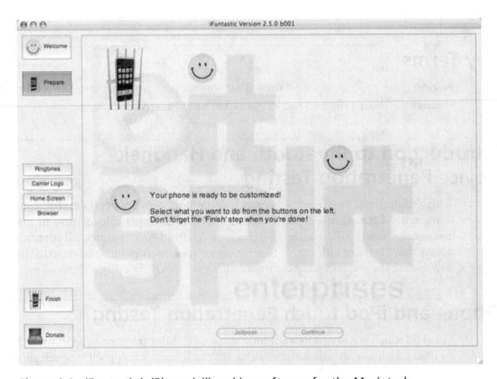

Figure 6-1   iFuntastic is iPhone jailbreaking software for the Macintosh.

AppSnapp

The procedure for jailbreaking using AppSnapp is as follows:

1. Go to *http://www.jailbreakme.com* on the iPhone.
2. At the bottom of the page, click the **Install AppSnapp** button.
3. Slide to unlock the iPhone.
4. Click the **Installer** icon on the iPhone, and then click **Sources** and install the Community Sources package.
5. Under System, install the BDS subsystem and openSSH.

iDemocracy

iDemocracy is an iPhone jailbreaking program for Windows. The program, shown in Figure 6-2, includes these features:

- A GUI interface with simple instructions
- Allows a user to perform command-line scripting
- Installs Installer.app, which in turn installs third-party applications
- Unlocks any SIM card using anySIM.app

iActivator

iActivator is a Cocoa-based jailbreaking application for the Macintosh. It uses a graphical interface, shown in Figure 6-3, and includes a feature to restore the phone to its original state before the jailbreak.

iNdependence

iNdependence (Figure 6-4) is another Cocoa-based application for Mac OS X, providing a simple interface for jailbreaking.

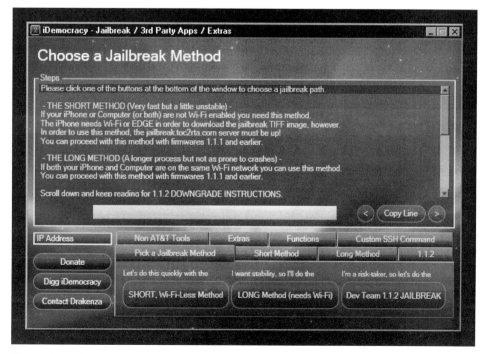

Figure 6-2   iDemocracy runs on a Windows machine and jailbreaks iPhones.

Source: http://www.iphone-hacks.com/2007/07/. Accessed 2007.

Figure 6-3   iActivator can restore an iPhone to its read-only state.

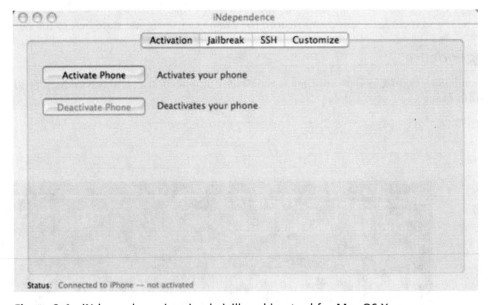

Figure 6-4   iNdependence is a simple jailbreaking tool for Mac OS X.

Step 2: Unlock the iPhone

By default, iPhones can only use the SIM cards of licensed carriers. However, if the iPhone is unlocked, it can use any SIM card. There are many online services that will unlock the iPhone after receiving the phone's unique 15-digit IMEI (International Mobile Equipment Identity), but they only work for a few hours. Tools such as iPhoneSimFree, iDemocracy, and anySIM, however, can permanently unlock the iPhone.

anySIM

anySIM (Figure 6-5) is a GUI-based SIM unlocking solution for iPhones. It is fully automatic after being installed to a jailbroken iPhone by following these steps:

1. Download anySIM 1.1 and extract it.
2. Move the anySIM file to the Applications folder.

Figure 6-5   anySIM can unlock an iPhone to allow it to use any SIM card.

3. Open the terminal (located in /Applications/Utilities) and type the following, where <IP address> is the iPhone's IP address:

```
scp -r /Applications/anySIM.app root@<IP address>:/Applications/
```

4. Restart the iPhone.
5. Run the anySIM application.

Step 3: Activate the Voice mail Button

After unlocking the iPhone, if the visual voice mail feature does not work, the tester can perform the following steps:

1. Find the voice mail number of the iPhone's carrier.
2. Dial the following number, where <voice mail number> is that voice mail number:

```
*5005*86*<voice mail number>#
```

3. Tap **call**.
4. Tap **voice mail**.

Step 4: Hack the iPhone Using Metasploit

The Metasploit tool can be used to scan for iPhone vulnerabilities, and it explains how to exploit those vulnerabilities. These vulnerabilities may allow the attacker to do the following:

- Take control of the iPhone to operate it remotely
- Gain root access to the iPhone

- Remotely access recently modified files
- Access stored e-mails
- View the iPhone's Web browsing history

Step 5: Check for Access Points with the Same Name and Encryption Type

Every wireless access point has an SSID, which is a 32-bit alphanumeric name. iPhones identify access points by their SSIDs. An attacker can create an access point with the same SSID and encryption type as a trusted one in order to fool iPhone users. The attacker can then set the access point to redirect users to a malicious Web page.

Step 6: Check Whether the iPhone Can Receive Malformed Data

iPhone system software 1.1.2 and 1.1.3 with Safari browser are vulnerable to DoS attacks. This browser has a design flaw that executes malicious scripts. The penetration tester should test for this flaw using the following method:

1. Extract the binaries from the iPhone either through jailbreaking or with the iPhoneInterface tool.
2. Analyze the binaries using a disassembler.
3. Perform a source code audit, and send this malformed data to the device to make it crash.
4. Alternatively, send an HTML page containing malicious JavaScript. Once the HTML page is opened by the user, it exploits the vulnerability, surrendering complete control of the device.
5. Try to extract information from the device such as:
   - Personal data
   - Passwords
   - E-mails
   - Browsing history

Step 7: Check Whether Basic Memory Mapping Information Can Be Extracted

The Mac OS X CrashReporter monitors programs for crashes. If a crash is detected, it records the logs of that crash along with relevant register values. This recorded information can be transmitted to the desktop computer during synchronization, or it can be downloaded from the iPhone by using jailbreaking software or the iPhoneInterface tool.

CrashReporter provides register values and basic memory information but does not provide direct access to memory. For getting direct access to memory or other crucial information, an iPhone can be modified so that applications will dump core files when they crash. To accomplish this, the file /etc/lauchd.conf with the line "limit core unlimited" must be added to the iPhone with iPhoneInterface. Using iPhoneInterface, core files can be obtained from the iPhone's /core directory. A debugger such as gdb is used to read these core files. An attacker can use this information to crash the iPhone.

BlackBerry Penetration Testing

The BlackBerry, a popular smartphone from Research In Motion (RIM), has the following known vulnerabilities:

- Files are sent to the BlackBerry as e-mail attachments from the BlackBerry Attachment Service. If TIFF image files are sent, it can cause a boundary error, interrupting service.
- While handling Server Routing Protocol (SRP) packets, some errors may interrupt the communication between the BlackBerry Enterprise Server and BlackBerry Router, resulting in DoS attacks.
- Malformed Microsoft Word (.doc) files in e-mail attachments can cause boundary errors. This vulnerability results in a buffer overflow, allowing attackers to execute arbitrary code.

Step 1: Blackjack

Blackjacking refers to hijacking a BlackBerry connection. Attackers use the BlackBerry as a conduit to bypass security settings and attack a network. This is usually done using the BBProxy tool. The attacker installs BBProxy on a user's BlackBerry or sends it as an e-mail attachment. When the tool is activated, it creates an encrypted channel between the attacker and the internal network.

Step 2: Send TIFF Image Files

Penetration testers can try to initiate an attack by sending TIFF image files to the device. The BlackBerry Attachment Service faces problems when managing TIFF image files, resulting in a DoS attack when the user opens the attached TIFF file.

PDA Penetration Testing

PDAs that use wireless services or wireless ports are vulnerable to wireless attacks. The best way to protect them from these attacks is to install a VPN client on the PDA.

Step 1: Crack the PDA Passwords

Testers can try to obtain the PDA's password using standard password-cracking techniques. Tools such as Brutus, Cain and Abel, and Hydra can be used for this purpose.

Step 2: Attempt ActiveSync Attacks

The most common attacks on PDAs are ActiveSync attacks. ActiveSync synchronizes Windows-based PDAs and smartphones to a desktop computer. ActiveSync is password protected, making it vulnerable to traditional dictionary and brute-force attacks. After obtaining the password, the attacker can steal private information or run malicious code, such as a keylogger or other spyware.

Step 3: Check Whether the IR Port Is Enabled

An infrared port is used to transfer data between two PDA devices over short distances. If the port is enabled, as shown in Figure 6-6, it means that device is vulnerable to attack. A tester can try to use the infrared port to send malicious software and access personal information.

Step 4: Check Whether Encrypted Data Can Be Decrypted

After gaining access to the personal information on the PDA, attempt to decrypt the data. Try cryptanalysis tools such as Crank and Jipher.

Bluetooth Penetration Testing

Bluetooth is a commonly used standard for short-range communication. Some of its uses include:

- Transferring data between a mobile device and a PC
- Connecting a printer, keyboard, or mouse to a PC
- Sending photos and ringtones from one device to another

These devices connect and communicate via short-range ad hoc networks known as *piconets*. Bluetooth attacks include the following:

- *Bluejacking*: Bluejacking does not involve hijacking any devices; it simply involves sending messages to devices over Bluetooth. This does not cause any damage, but can irritate victims and disrupt their operations. Bluejacking works because of small loopholes in the initialization stage of the Bluetooth communication protocol. Bluetooth devices exchange information at the time of the first connection, before allowing any communication. When this happens, the initiating Bluetooth device's name must be shown on the other device's screen. This name could simply be an unsolicited message.

- *Bluespam*: Bluespam is a technique in which an attacker finds other Bluetooth devices and sends files to them using the object exchange (OBEX) protocol.

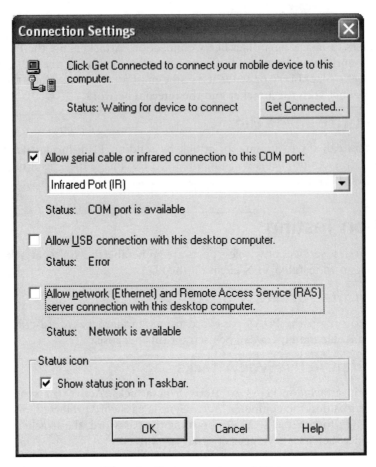

Figure 6-6 Enabling the IR port can leave a PDA open to attacks.

- *Bluesnarfing*: A Bluesnarfing attack is used to access sensitive data through a Bluetooth device. The attacker exploits a vulnerability in the implementation of the OBEX protocol. Improper implementation of device firmware can allow an attacker to retrieve files by guessing their names. Other devices such as laptops, PDAs, and desktop computers are also vulnerable to this attack.

- *Bluebug:* The Bluebug technique exploits a security loophole in Bluetooth-enabled devices in order to access private and confidential information from the victim's device.

- *Short pairing code*: *Pairing* is the process of associating Bluetooth devices with one another so that they can communicate. These devices share secrets that are used for future communication. A pairing attack is possible if this pairing process is eavesdropped. The attacker acts as one of the two devices and sends a message to the other device, saying that the device has forgotten the link key. This message prompts the other device to discard the key and create a new pairing session, pairing it with the attacker's device.

- *Man-in-the-middle attacks*: A man-in-the-middle (MITM) attack occurs when the attacker has the link keys and unit keys (BD_ADDR) of the Bluetooth devices, allowing him or her to eavesdrop on the conversation between the devices. The attacker pretends to be both the devices, so the victims are unaware that the attacker exists. The attacker can then send malicious packets to one or both users.

- *BTKeylogging*: A BTKeylogging attack can be performed if the target keyboard has a fixed PIN code and the attacker knows its BD_ADDR. The attacker can launch a PIN cracking attack to discover the fixed PIN code of the target Bluetooth keyboard, but he or she must know the initial pairing process between the target keyboard and the target computer. The attacker then intercepts all packets sent from the keyboard and records them.

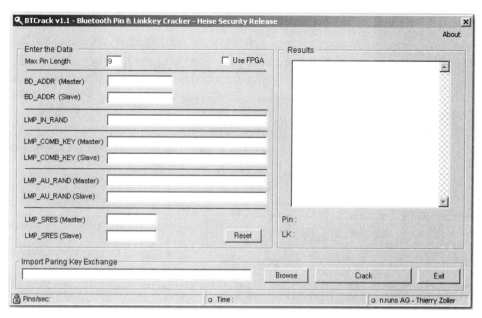

Figure 6-7   BTCrack cracks a Bluetooth device's PIN and link key.

- *Blueprinting*: Blueprinting is used to access details about Bluetooth devices remotely. This can help identify vulnerabilities. All Bluetooth-enabled devices have characteristics that are either unique or model specific. Blueprinting uses basic information revealed by the devices to determine the manufacturer and the device model.

- *Bluesmacking*: Bluetooth devices can only handle packets up to a certain size. In a Bluesmacking attack, the attacker creates a data packet larger than the allowable size and sends it to the victim's device. This causes a buffer overflow on the device and allows the attacker to execute malicious code.

Step 1: Crack the PIN

In this step, testers try to crack the PIN of the Bluetooth device. Brute-force algorithms, such as selection sort, can be used to find the PIN. This PIN can also be cracked using some password crackers such as Brutus and Hydra or sniffed during the pairing process.

BTCrack, shown in Figure 6-7, cracks the PIN and link key used in the pairing process. With this PIN, the attacker can authenticate against the device in the pairing process. An attacker can then use the link key to decrypt the data stream between the devices.

Step 2: Perform a Blueprinting Attack

A Blueprinting attack can help testers gain information that will lead to the discovery of vulnerabilities. Testers can use tools such as Blueprint and BTScanner to extract details such as:

- Bluetooth device address (BD_ADDR)
- Service description records
- Model of the device

Step 3: Extract SDP Profiles

Using Service Discovery Profiles (SDP), penetration testers can try to find details about services that Bluetooth devices offer one another. They can make use of tools such as sdptool and BTScanner.

Step 4: Attempt Pairing Code Attacks

Testers can perform a pairing attack by eavesdropping on the pairing process between two devices. The tester's device can perform a MITM or session hijack attack to act as one of the devices and send a message to the other device saying that the link key was lost. A new pairing session will then be started with a new key.

Step 5: Attempt a Man-In-The-Middle Attack

Penetration testers can try an MITM attack by making independent connections with victims. They can then obtain the link keys (secret keys) and unit keys (BD_ADDR) of the Bluetooth devices. Testers then interrupt the communication between the two victims and initiate a connection with each of them, acting as the other. Finally, the testers can relay messages between the users making them think they are talking to each other directly.

Step 6: Attempt a Bluejacking Attack

To perform a Bluejacking attack, testers must first modify security settings using the following steps:

1. Right-click on the **Bluetooth** icon in the taskbar.
2. Select **Advanced Configuration**, and click the **Client Applications** tab.
3. Select **PIM Item Transfer** and then **Properties**.
4. Uncheck the **Secure Connection** check box.

To attempt the attack, testers follow these steps:

1. Open the Address Book in Outlook Express, right-click on a contact, and then click **Properties**.
2. Select the **Name** tab, modify the contact details, and then click the **OK** button.
3. Right-click on the contact and select **Action**, then **Send to Bluetooth**, and finally **Other**.
4. Select the Bluetooth device, and then click **Send**.

Step 7: Attempt a BTKeylogging Attack

A BTKeylogging attack can be performed if the target keyboard has a fixed PIN code and the attacker knows its BD_ADDR. Testers can use a protocol analyzer to intercept the required information (IN_RAND, LK_RAND, AU_RAND, SRES, and EN_RAND) to perform the attack. Then, they can intercept all packets coming from the keyboard and decrypt them.

Step 8: Attempt Bluesmacking (Ping of Death)

In this step, testers create a data packet larger than the Bluetooth device can handle. This may cause an overflow. Testers can then try to perform some malicious actions on the device after sending the packet.

Step 9: Attempt a Bluesnarfing Attack

A Bluesnarfing attack accesses data from nearby Bluetooth-enabled devices by exploiting vulnerabilities in the implementation of the object exchange (OBEX) protocol. Devices such as laptops, PDAs, and desktop computers are vulnerable to this attack.

Testers can use the BlueSnarfer tool, shown in Figure 6-8, to access details such as:

- Calendar
- Contact list
- E-mail
- Text messages

Step 10: Attempt a Bluebug Attack

The testing team can use the Bluediving tool, which exploits loopholes in Bluetooth, to perform a Bluebug attack. This helps in accessing Bluetooth devices without authorization. After gaining access, testers can attempt to do the following:

- Initiate a phone call
- Send an SMS
- Read SMS from the phone
- Read and write contact list entries
- Set call forwarding rules
- Make an Internet connection

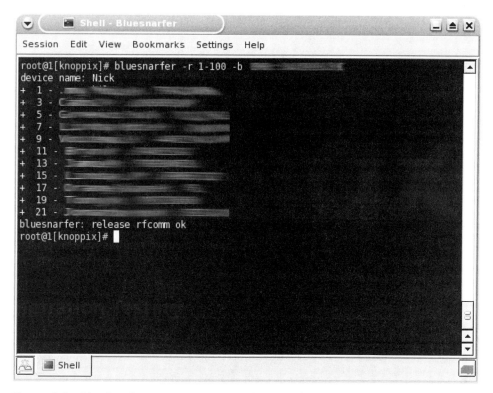

Figure 6-8   BlueSnarfer can access personal details from nearby Bluetooth devices.

Step 11: Attempt Bluespam

To attempt a Bluespam attack, testers can use a Palm PDA with an SD or MMC card. They then create the directory /PALM/programs/BlueSpam/Send/, put the Bluespam file in it, and then send that file to the victim's Bluetooth device. If Bluespam finds any Palm PDAs in discoverable and connectable mode, it stops all connection attempts and sends messages back to the sender.

Chapter Summary

- Jailbreaking is the process of unlocking an iPhone or iPod touch to permit the install unlicensed applications, add new ringtones, or change the device's wallpaper. This also makes the file system readable by a computer.
- Unlocking an iPhone allows it to use any SIM card.
- Once a PDA is compromised, personal information can be accessed from the device.
- Blackjacking is a method of hijacking BlackBerry connections.
- ActiveSync synchronizes Windows-based PDAs and smartphones with a desktop computer.
- Pairing is the process of two Bluetooth devices associating with one another.
- Bluesnarfing is used to access sensitive data through a Bluetooth device.
- Blueprinting is used to access details about Bluetooth devices remotely.
- Bluespam can find Bluetooth-enabled devices and send spam files using the OBEX protocol.
- The Bluediving penetration testing tool exploits loopholes in Bluetooth and performs a Bluebug attack.
- A BTKeylogging attack can be performed if the target keyboard has a fixed PIN code and the attacker knows its BD_ADDR.

## Chapter 7

Telecommunication and Broadband Communication Penetration Testing

Objectives

After completing this chapter, you should be able to:

- Check for firewalls
- Test firewalls
- Configure Web browsers for enhanced security
- Disable cookies
- Protect against scripting attacks
- Test antivirus and antispyware software
- Check for wiretapping
- Check for WEP

Key Terms

ActiveX   a technology developed by Microsoft that allows software applets to be reused in various applications

Browser plug-in   software that extends the capabilities of a browser

Cookie   a piece of information sent by a Web site to a browser when the site is accessed

Firewall   a hardware device or software running on a computer that monitors the network traffic passing through it and denies or allows traffic based on previously defined rules and configurations

Spyware   stealthy computer monitoring software that allows an attacker to secretly record all activities of a targeted user over a network

Stealth mode   a general term for a process operating with deliberate secrecy or camouflage to avoid detection by different scanning tools

Virtual private network (VPN)   a network tunneled through other networks, dedicated to specific communications

Web browser   an application that allows a user to view Web pages

Wiretapping   the act of monitoring telephone and Internet communications without the knowledge of the target

Introduction to Telecommunication and Broadband Communication Penetration Testing

The communication technologies through which different companies access the Internet have become indispensable to modern business practices. Broadband communication can be obtained over cable modem or digital subscriber line (DSL), or through satellite broadband service. Cable modem networks make use of the unused capacity of television bandwidth to provide Internet access. DSL networks provide Internet access over telephone lines, and satellite broadband service provides access through satellites.

Use of these communication technologies can also make networks vulnerable, however. The speed and ease of use that broadband brings also makes it easier to conduct attacks against networks. Because many employees access company networks from locations such as the home or through public networks, the company's network is exposed to a variety of vulnerabilities. This chapter covers different ways to perform penetration testing on these networks.

Risks in Broadband Communication

Broadband communication provides fast access to information. Some features of this communication make it vulnerable to attack. The "always on" feature makes the systems and the network vulnerable, as it can lead to unauthorized access of information. Dial-up ISPs provide a new IP address for every connection. Since broadband is always on, the IP address remains the same allowing an attacker to easily attack the targeted system. Certain steps should be taken to ensure that communications are conducted safely and securely.

Steps for Broadband Communication Penetration Testing

The following steps should be followed for broadband communication penetration testing:

- *Step 1*: Check to see if a firewall device is installed on the network.
- *Step 2*: Check to see if Web browsers are properly configured.
- *Step 3*: Check for operating system configuration options.
- *Step 4*: Check for wireless and other home networking technologies.

Step 1: Check to See If a Firewall Device Is Installed on the Network

A *firewall* is a hardware device or software running on a computer that monitors the network traffic passing through it and denies or allows traffic based on previously defined rules and configurations. Every home network connected to a corporate network via a broadband connection should have a firewall installed.

The following steps should be used to test a network's firewall:

- *Step 1-1*: Check to see if personal or hardware firewalls are installed.
- *Step 1-2*: Check to see if these firewalls prevent intruders or detect any rogue software.
- *Step 1-3*: Check to see if logging is enabled on the firewall.
- *Step 1-4*: Check to see if the firewall is in stealth mode.

Step 1-1: Check to See If Personal or Hardware Firewalls Are Installed   A personal firewall installed on a system provides security to the user's system, while a hardware firewall that is in between the broadband connection and the user's system offers security to the network, as shown in Figure 7-1. To protect the network and all systems, it is necessary to install both types of firewalls. Penetration testers should check to see if these firewalls are working properly.

Figure 7-1   Firewalls can be configured to block dangerous Web sites.

Step 1-2: Check to See If These Firewalls Prevent Intruders or Detect Any Rogue Software   There are many techniques and tools available to attack a system. Some tools are powerful enough to easily bypass firewalls. A well-configured firewall will ensure a secure system.

Testers should check to see if these firewalls prevent intruders or detect software that sends important data from the company's network to an external system. To do this, they can try to send a known harmless virus or Trojan into the network. If this virus or Trojan is not detected, then the firewall is vulnerable to attack. Testers need to make sure that the virus or Trojan is one that would not disrupt system operations if it passed through the firewall.

Step 1-3: Check to See If Logging Is Enabled on the Firewall   Logging is necessary to keep track of the operations of the firewall. Logging must be actively enabled to be used. Testers should check to see if logging is enabled on the firewall. If the logging is disabled, intrusion attempts will go unnoticed.

Step 1-4: Check to See If the Firewall Is in Stealth Mode   *Stealth mode* is a general term for a process operating with deliberate secrecy or camouflage to avoid detection by different scanning tools. Testers should check the firewall configuration to see if the firewall is in stealth mode. If it is in stealth mode, systems will not respond to connection attempts and will appear as if they are not on the network.

Step 2: Check to See If Web Browsers Are Properly Configured

A *Web browser* is an application that allows users to view Web pages. It plays an important role in Internet communication. Attackers can attack a network if Web browsers are not properly configured. So, to protect Internet communication, it is necessary to check the Web browser's configuration. Penetration testers can use the following steps to test Web browsers:

- *Step 2-1*: Check to see if the browser has the default configuration.
- *Step 2-2*: Check for browser plug-ins.
- *Step 2-3*: Check to see if active code is enabled.
- *Step 2-4*: Check to see if the browser version is updated.
- *Step 2-5*: Check to see if cookies are enabled.
- *Step 2-6*: Check to see if scripting languages are enabled.

Step 2-1: Check to See If the Browser Has the Default Configuration   Most users keep their browser's security setting at the default level. This default configuration may leave the browser vulnerable to attack. Testers should check to see if the security level of the Web browser is set to the default level. The following procedure is used to check a browser's security settings (Figure 7-2):

1. Open the browser.
2. Click **Tools**.
3. Click **Internet**.
4. Click **Options**.
5. Click **Security**.

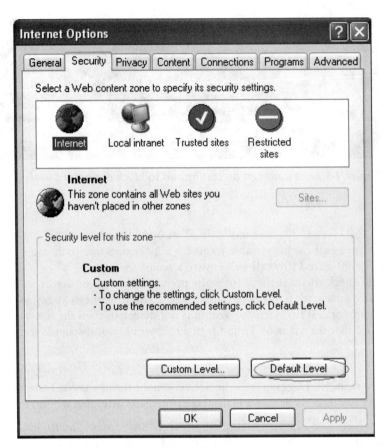

Figure 7-2 The security setting of a Web browser should not be at the default level.

Step 2-2: Check for Browser Plug-Ins A *browser plug-in* is software that extends the capabilities of the browser (e.g., the ability to download and display video, hear audio, or play animations). These plug-ins are sometimes vulnerable to attack. Therefore, the number of plug-ins should be limited based on necessity. Testers should check to see if the installed plug-ins are from trusted sites.

Step 2-3: Check to See If Active Code Is Enabled **ActiveX** is a technology developed by Microsoft that allows software applets to be reused in various applications. ActiveX controls are often vulnerable to attack. Enabling these controls provides an attacker with the chance to attack the network. ActiveX should only be enabled when required. Testers can use the following steps to check whether ActiveX is enabled in a browser:

1. Open the browser.
2. Click **Tools**.
3. Click **Options**.
4. Click **Security**.
5. Select **Internet Custom** level.
6. Search for ActiveX controls and check to see whether they are enabled or disabled (Figure 7-3).

Step 2-4: Check to See If the Browser Version Is Updated Hackers are constantly discovering new vulnerabilities in browsers, so companies have to respond by updating their browsers to remove these vulnerabilities. Use of old-version browsers gives an attacker the chance to exploit outdated vulnerabilities. To protect the network from such attacks, testers should check to see if the browser is the latest version. They should also check to see if the automatic update option is enabled (Figure 7-4).

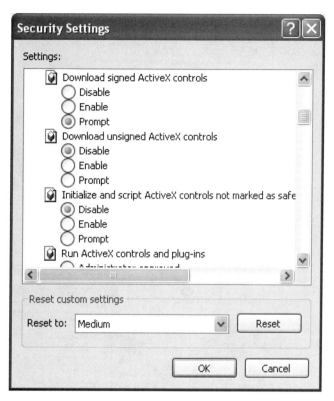

Figure 7-3   ActiveX should be kept in the disabled state.

Figure 7-4   Web browsers should be kept up to date.

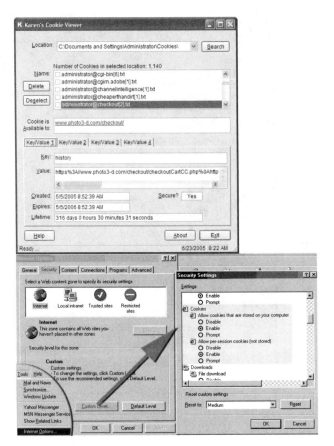

Figure 7-5 Cookies should be disabled to protect against attacks.

Step 2-5: Check to See If Cookies Are Enabled A *cookie* is a piece of information sent by a Web site to the browser when the site is accessed. It is saved to the hard drive and records information about the parts of the Web site visited and other information about the user, such as usernames and passwords. Attackers can steal cookies and learn important information from them. To protect against such attacks, users should disable cookies or clear the private data before closing the browser, as shown in Figure 7-5.

Testers should try to read the cookies from the browser, or use a tool such as a cookie viewer to view the content of the cookies. If these cookies can be viewed, it means they are not safe and are vulnerable to attack.

Step 2-6: Check to See If Scripting Languages Are Enabled Scripting languages such as JavaScript and VBScript are vulnerable to attack. Attackers can modify scripts and send malicious scripts to a user's computer. Malicious scripts can also be embedded in Web sites that an attacker sets up. Often, attackers set up such Web sites to look like legitimate Web sites, thus tricking users into running these malicious scripts.

Testers can use the following steps to check whether scripting languages are enabled:

1. Open the browser.
2. Click **Tools**.
3. Click **Internet**.
4. Click **Options**.
5. Click **Security**.
6. Select **Internet Custom** level.
7. Search for scripting options and check whether scripts are enabled (Figure 7-6).

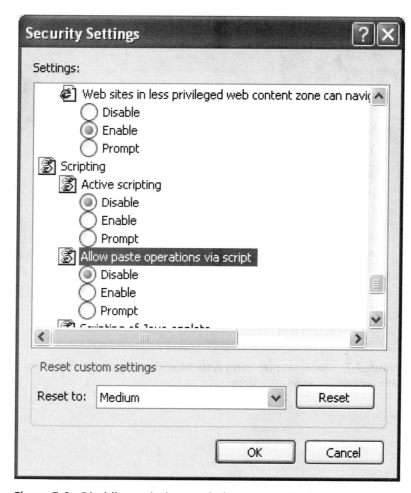

Figure 7-6   Disabling scripting can help prevent attacks.

Step 3: Check for Operating System Configuration Options

- *Step 3-1*: Check to see if the operating system and application software are updated.
- *Step 3-2*: Check to see if the file and printer sharing option is enabled.
- *Step 3-3*: Check to see if antivirus programs are enabled.
- *Step 3-4*: Check the configuration of antivirus programs.
- *Step 3-5*: Check to see if antispyware software is enabled.

Step 3-1: Check to See If the Operating System and Application Software Are Updated Operating systems and application software are also vulnerable to attack. Many older versions of software contain vulnerabilities. Vendors of this software develop new versions to remove those vulnerabilities. To keep the OS and application software secure from attack, it is necessary to use the latest versions (Figure 7-7).

Step 3-2: Check to See If the File and Printer Sharing Option Is Enabled File sharing can make a system vulnerable. An attacker can send malicious files containing viruses through the file sharing option. In the same way, printer sharing can also be an avenue for attack. Performing the following steps can protect a system from this type of attack:

1. Check to see if the file and printer sharing option is enabled.
2. If not, go to the Control Panel and select **Printers and Faxes**.
3. Select any printer, right-click, and select **Sharing**

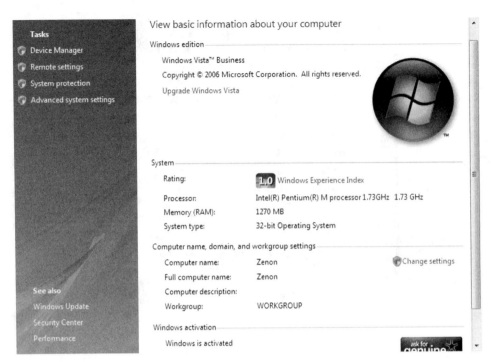

Figure 7-7   Updating operating systems and applications is an important part of maintaining a secure system.

4. Try to access files and printers on this system over the network.

5. If the files or printers can be accessed, it means the system is vulnerable to attack. Turn off file and printer sharing if the system is vulnerable.

Step 3-3: Check to See If Antivirus Programs Are Enabled Antivirus software is specifically designed to detect viruses. A virus scanner is an important piece of software and should be installed on every PC. If there is no scanner, the chances are high that a virus will hit the system. A virus protector should be run regularly on PCs, and the scan engine and virus signature database should be updated often (Figure 7-8).

Penetration testers should check to see if the antivirus programs are enabled on systems. They can send a virus to the system and check whether the antivirus program catches it, as shown in Figure 7-9. If the virus is not detected, the system is vulnerable to attack.

Step 3-4: Check the Configuration of Antivirus Programs Antivirus programs, which should be updated often, are important in keeping a check on data passing through a system. Users are warned of a possible virus infection if malicious data are detected. However, antivirus programs must be configured properly to use them to their fullest extent. They should be configured to scan all incoming files and e-mails. This can be tested by sending e-mail containing a malicious attachment and checking to see if the antivirus program detects it.

Step 3-5: Check to See If Antispyware Software Is Enabled *Spyware* is stealthy computer monitoring software that allows an attacker to secretly record all activities of a targeted user over the network. Spyware detectors are used to detect spyware present on a system.

Testers can check to see if antispyware software is enabled and functioning properly by sending spyware to the system (Figure 7-10). If the spyware is not detected, it means the system may be vulnerable to attack.

Step 4: Check for Wireless and Other Home Networking Technologies

- *Step 4-1*: Check for VPN policy configurations.
- *Step 4-2*: Attempt wiretapping.
- *Step 4-3*: Try to perform wardriving.

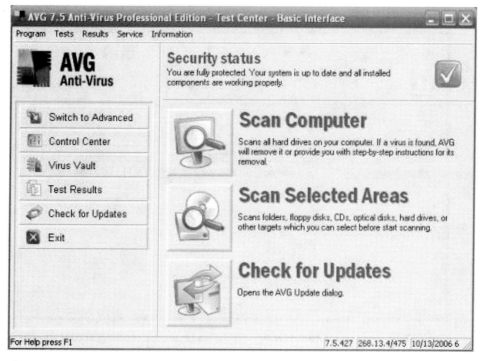

Figure 7-8   Antivirus software should be updated regularly.

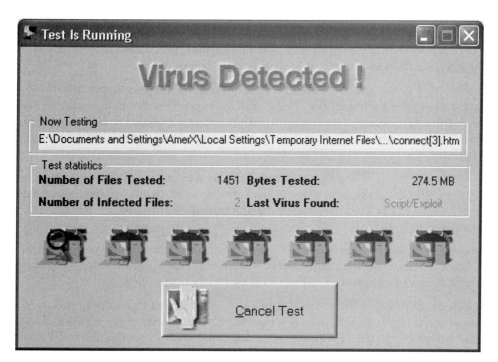

Figure 7-9   Testing a system with an actual virus is a good way to ensure security.

- *Step 4-4*: Check to see if the wireless base station is using the default configuration.
- *Step 4-5*: Check to see if WEP is implemented.
- *Step 4-6*: Try to crack the WEP key.
- *Step 4-7*: Try to crack the SSID.
- *Step 4-8*: Check to see if the Simple Network Management Protocol (SNMP) is enabled.

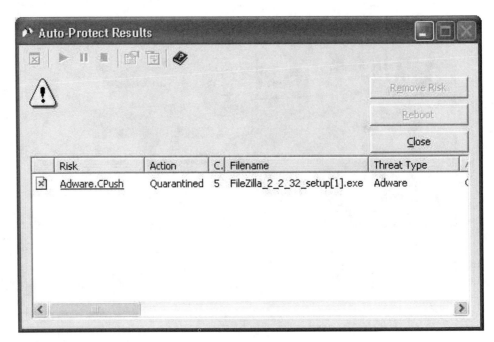

Figure 7-10   Antispyware software should be tested by sending actual spyware to the system.

Step 4-1: Check for VPN Policy Configurations A *virtual private network (VPN)* is a network tunneled through other networks, dedicated to specific communications. Penetration testers should check the configurations of any VPNs on the network to ensure that they are secure.

Step 4-2: Attempt Wiretapping Monitoring telephone and Internet communications without the knowledge of the target is called *wiretapping*. There are two types of wiretapping: passive and active. In passive wiretapping, a third party simply captures information, whereas in active wiretapping, the third party actually alters it. Testers can use software tools such as Wiretapping Professional and WireTap Pro to test for wiretapping vulnerabilities.

Step 4-3: Try to Perform Wardriving Wardriving, also called access point mapping, is the act of locating and possibly exploiting connections to wireless local area networks while driving around a geographic location. Testers can use tools such as WarLinux and AirFart to attempt wardriving.

Step 4-4: Check to See If the Wireless Base Station Is Using the Default Configuration Testers should check if the wireless base station is using the default configuration. Typically, the default configuration is not secure. Most wireless base stations use default passwords that are easily discovered on the Internet. Testers can try these passwords to attempt to connect to the wireless base station.

Step 4-5: Check to See If WEP Is Implemented WEP (Wired Equivalent Privacy) is a security protocol used in many wireless local area networks. It is used to provide security to the network. Testers can use software tools such as NetStumbler to see if a wireless network is using WEP for encryption. If WEP is being used, it shows a circle to the left of the MAC address, which has a picture of a small lock inside it, as shown in Figure 7-11.

Step 4-6: Try to Crack the WEP Key A WEP key is a hexadecimal security code that protects Wi-Fi networks. These keys help exchange encoded messages between the devices on a local network. An attacker can attack the network by cracking the WEP key. Testers can try to crack the WEP key using WEP key-cracking tools such as Aircrack and WEPCrack. If the WEP key can be cracked, it implies that the network is not secure with WEP. Testers should try an encryption scheme such as WPA or WPA2 to secure the network, and retest.

Step 4-7: Try to Crack the SSID A service set ID (SSID) is the sequence of characters that is attached to each packet transmitted on a wireless network and identifies that network. The SSID can contain a maximum

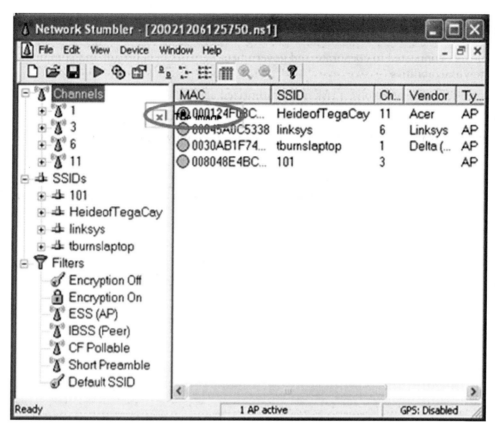

Figure 7-11   If WEP is being used, NetStumbler shows a circle to the left of the MAC address, which has a picture of a small lock inside it.

Figure 7-12   An SNMP ping tool can detect whether SNMP is enabled.

of 32 alphanumeric characters. All wireless devices that communicate with each other have the same SSID. Most wireless base stations give the user the option of broadcasting the SSID, thus giving an attacker a vital piece of information. Even with this feature switched off, it is possible for an attacker to discover the SSID. Testers should use tools such as Cain & Abel and Hydra to attempt to discover the SSID.

Step 4-8: Check to See If the Simple Network Management Protocol (SNMP) Is Enabled   Wireless base stations make use of Simple Network Management Protocol (SNMP) to monitor network devices. Testers can check to see if SNMP is enabled or disabled by using an SNMP ping tool, as shown in Figure 7-12.

Chapter Summary

- Employees connected to corporate and government networks via broadband communication may create vulnerabilities.
- Internet connections involve a risk of unauthorized access.
- Use stronger encryption, such as WPA or WPA2, to secure data if WEP can be cracked.
- Spyware is stealthy computer monitoring software that allows an attacker to secretly record all activities of a user over the network.
- Antivirus software is specifically designed to detect viruses.
- File sharing can affect a system; an attacker can send any malicious files containing viruses, which in turn affect the system over the network.

Index